RES GESTAE DIVI AUGUSTI

as recorded in the
Monumentum Ancyranum
and the
Monumentum Antiochenum

D0939298

Introduction
Grammatical Notes
Historical Commentary
Facing Vocabulary

Rex Wallace

Bolchazy-Carducci Publishers, Inc.
Wauconda, Illinois

General Editor
Laurie Haight Keenan

Contributing Editors
Aaron Baker
Allan Kershaw

Cover Illustration
Cameo of Augustus set into cross of Lothair

Cover Design
Charlene M. Hernandez

© 2000 Bolchazy-Carducci Publishers, Inc.
All Rights Reserved

Bolchazy-Carducci Publishers, Inc.
1000 Brown Street
Wauconda, IL 60084 USA
www.bolchazy.com

Printed in the United States of America
2007
by BookSurge

ISBN 978-0-86516-455-0

Library of Congress Cataloging-in-Publication Data

Augustus, Emperor or Rome, 63 B.C.-14 A.D.
    Res gestae divi Augusti : as recorded in the Monumentum ancyranum and the
Monumentum antichenum : introduction, grammatical notes, historical commentary,
facing vocabulary / edited by Rex Wallace.
        p.   cm.
    Text in Latin; pref., introd, and notes in English.
    Includes bibliographical references (p.) and index.
    ISBN 0-86516-455-x (pbk. : alk. paper)
    1. Rome—History—Augustus, 30 B.C.-14 A.D. I. Wallace, Rex. II. Title.

DG279 .A928 1999
937'.07—dc21   99-054526

in memoriam
William J. Sheehan

CONTENTS

PREFACE

I endorse the idea that students who are just beginning to read Latin benefit from texts that enable them to read large chunks of the language without having to struggle to look up a great number of words in the dictionary. I also believe that these students profit—in the initial stages of their reading—by having access to detailed grammatical commentary. This book is designed to accommodate the student in both of these areas. Vocabulary, vocabulary notes, grammatical commentary, and text are on facing pages.

Introductory texts of the sort endorsed here are, as far as I am aware, concerned with literary Latin. This is to be expected, inasmuch as the ultimate aim of most Latin courses is to equip students with the ability to read and appreciate the Latin of some of western literature's greatest writers. But there is another world of Latin out there, one that is intrinsically interesting, one that some students find absolutely fascinating, and one that students have very little exposure to, even if they are enrolled as majors or minors in undergraduate Classics programs, namely the world of Latin inscriptions. One of the aims of this text is to open this world to beginning Latin students. What better place to begin than with the "queen" of Latin inscriptions, the *Res Gestae* of the emperor Augustus. As a historical document, it is of unsurpassed significance. And its Latin is so straightforward and to the point that students who are beginning to read Latin prose can, with a minimum of grammatical assistance and a handful of historical notes, read and understand this important document.

The text printed in this book is basically that published in the third edition of Jean Gagé's *Res Gestae Divi Augusti* (for full reference see bibliography at the end of the Introduction). I have stripped the text of the epigraphic conventions and have eliminated also the conventions employed by Gagé to indicate the textual authority for problematic readings. Instructors who wish to review the problems of restoring the text should consult Gagé. I have also had occasion to make changes in punctuation and have added, as is customary in texts aimed at beginning Latin students, macrons over long vowels. My guide for vowel length is Alfred Ernout and Antoine Meillet,

Dictionnaire étymologique de la langue latine, 1985, 4th ed., Paris: Klincksieck.

For historical commentary I have relied chiefly on Brunt & Moore's *Res Gestae Divi Augusti: The Achievements of the Divine Augustus; The Cambridge Ancient History, Vol. X;* Ronald Syme's *The Roman Revolution;* and on other modern works on Augustus and the Augustan Age, for which I refer the reader to the bibliography appended to the introduction of this text.

The running vocabulary on the pages facing the Latin text consists primarily of words not found in *Ecce Romani,* levels I and II. Generally, the first instance of a vocabulary item is entered in the list, but subsequent occurrences are not. On a few occasions repeated vocabulary items have significantly different meanings, in which case these words are listed a second time. All vocabulary items appear in the vocabulary list at the end of the book.

I taught a preliminary version of the text in an introductory Latin prose course in 1995. More recently my colleague, Gilbert Lawall, taught this text in his intensive Latin course as a final reading project. He supplemented it with outside readings, in particular the historical notes in Brunt and Moore (*op. cit.*), a combination that he thought the students found particularly satisfying.

I am indebted to Gilbert Lawall, of the University of Massachusetts, for his comments on the historical and grammatical notes to this text. I also thank Charles Babcock, of The Ohio State University, for reading an earlier version of the text and for offering many suggestions for improvement. The photographs printed here are from the archive of epigraphical photographs housed at the Center for Epigraphical and Palaeographical Studies, The Ohio State University. I thank the Center for granting me permission to use them. The maps were redrawn and then edited by Tim Pieri, a student in Classics at the University of Massachusetts.

Rex E. Wallace
University of Massachusetts
July 1999

GRAMMATICAL ABBREVIATIONS

nom.	nominative
gen.	genitive
dat.	dative
acc.	accusative
abl.	ablative
m.	masculine
f.	feminine
n.	neuter
sg.	singular
pl.	plural
adj.	adjective
adv.	adverb
conj.	conjunction
indecl.	indeclinable
indef.	indefinite
inf.	infinitve
irreg.	irregular
prep.	preposition
pro.	pronoun
rel.	relative
subj.	subjunctive
1st	1st person
2nd	2nd person
3rd	3rd person
perf.	perfect
act.	active
pass.	passive
inf.	infinitive

INTRODUCTION

§1. Res Gestae

Shortly after the emperor Augustus died (August 19, A.D. 14), the Vestal Virgins made public in the Senate four documents that Augustus had entrusted to them for safekeeping: his last will and testament, directions for his funeral, an accounting of the finances of the empire, and a description of his accomplishments, his *Res Gestae*. Augustus directed his heirs to inscribe this last document on bronze tablets and then to set the tablets up in front of his Mausoleum on the Campus Martius. The original bronze tablets have not survived, but copies of the text have, in the form of inscriptions that were set up in the Roman province of Galatia (in modern Turkey). These inscriptions form the basis of our text of the *Res Gestae* of the emperor Augustus.

§1.1 Versions of the Inscription

The text is preserved in two versions, one Latin and one Greek. The most important copy of the Latin version, the so-called *Monumentum Ancyranum*, was inscribed in six columns on two interior walls of the *pronaos* of the temple of Rome and Augustus at Ancyra (modern Ankara), the capital of Roman Galatia (see Figs. 1 and 2). This version is reasonably well preserved, although part of the wall of the *pronaos* containing the inscription has been damaged and as a result sections of the inscription have been lost (see Fig. 3). Fortunately, another version of the *Res Gestae*, the *Monumentum Antiochenum*, was found at the city of Antioch in the region of Pisidia (close to modern Yalvaç). Although this inscription is also fragmentary, the Latin of this text is preserved in places where it is not preserved in the *Monumentum Ancyranum*. By combining the readings attested in the two Latin versions it is possible to restore the text to something close to its original condition. It is worth noting, however, that the inscription found at Antioch is not quite the same as that found at Ancyra. The two Latin versions are in all probability copies made from the same model, presumably the one carried from Rome into the provinces.

The most important Greek version of the *Res Gestae* is a translation of the *Monumentum Ancyranum*. It was inscribed on the exterior wall of the *cella* of the temple of Rome and Augustus at Ancyra (see Fig. 2). The Greek version has fewer lacunae than the Latin version, and so it is possible to check the content of troublesome Latin passages against the Greek. In several instances the only surviving portion of the text is that of the Greek inscription. In these cases the Latin text has been supplied from the Greek by modern editors.

Another version of the Greek text was found in Pisidian Apollonia, also located in the territory of Galatia. Unfortunately, this version has survived only in fragments.

§1.2 Date, Preamble, and Form

The date of composition of the *Res Gestae* is a matter of considerable dispute. Some authorities argue that the text was written at various stages during Augustus' life. Others argue that it was composed at some point in the middle of Augustus' career and then periodically updated. Still others argue that the *Res Gestae* speaks for itself. In the final paragraph (35) Augustus says, "I was in my seventy-sixth year when I composed this." By this reckoning, the composition of the *Res Gestae* can be placed between Augustus' last birthday, which was September 23, A.D. 13, and the date of his death, August 19, A.D. 14.

The preamble of the *Res Gestae* cannot have been in the form that we have it on the inscriptions. The word **exemplar** and the reference to Rome (line 3) show that at least the final portion of the preamble (after **fēcit**) was added for the benefit of provincial readers. It is possible—though it cannot be proven or disproved—that the initial portion of the preamble (to **fēcit**) was not composed by the emperor Augustus but was added by Tiberius or under Tiberius' orders before a copy of the text was dispatched to the provinces.

As noted above, the *Monumentum Ancyranum* was incised in six columns on two interior walls of the temple of Rome and Augustus. The preamble was set off from the body of the inscription by the size and the formality of its letters (see Fig. 3). The body of the inscription was divided into 35 paragraphs and each paragraph was set off from the others by extending the first letter over into the lefthand margin of the text. The ends of most paragraphs were formally marked by means of a sign that had the shape of a staff. The punctuation at the end of sentences had various shapes: sometimes an oblique line, sometimes a sign resembling the number 3. Divisions between words were usually indicated by interpuncts set at mid-line level, but these were sometimes omitted between monosyllabic prepositions and the nouns they governed. Features of punctuation are visible in the photographs of the *Monumentum Ancyranum* (see Figs. 3, 4, and 5).

§1.3 Content and Organization

Authorities agree that it is difficult to classify the *Res Gestae* according to the epigraphic categories typically recognized for Latin inscriptions. The *Res Gestae* cannot be described as a funerary inscription or an honorary inscription. And it is not autobiography or history. Rather, it is all of the above. And more. The *Res Gestae* is Augustus' depiction of how he wished posterity to view him and the high points of his reign: as victorious general and wise statesman, as generous benefactor of the Roman state and people, as sponsor of Rome's architectural resurrection, and as modest recipient of countless honors from the Roman Senate and plebs.

The *Res Gestae* is organized by theme roughly into five sections. Section one (paragraphs 1–3) is a summary of Augustus' political and military activities from the beginning of his career (44 B.C.) up to 28 B.C. Section two (paragraphs 4–14) is a description of the honors bestowed upon Augustus by the Roman Senate and people. The third section (paragraphs 15–24) documents the personal expenses Augustus incurred through gratuities distributed to the army and the plebs and through the construction and repair of public buildings. The fourth section (paragraphs 25–33) describes Augustus' military achievements in Roman provinces and his diplomatic victories in foreign affairs. The concluding paragraphs (34 and 35) return to the themes of sections 1 and 2: political achievements and honors. They document the "restoration" of the Roman Republic in 28–27 B.C. and the senatorial decrees by which Octavian received the cognomen "Augustus" and the title *pater patriae*, "father of my country."

Greater light can be shed on the details of this organizational structure if each section of the text is set out in outline form:

The *Res Gestae* is an important document first and foremost because of what it tells us about the career of Augustus. But if we regard this inscription merely as a narrative of Augustus' achievements, then we miss an important point about the text's function. This is Augustus putting his spin on the important events of his career. He has selected, organized, and crafted the material presented in the *Res Gestae* as effectively as any contemporary political spinmeister. This means that we are required not only to read the text but also to read between its lines. Since the *Res Gestae* was intended for public consumption, it is unlikely that Augustus composed anything patently false. But at the same time we can point to numerous instances where Augustus has been less than forthcoming.

Augustus describes his rise to power in minimalist terms. He raised an army out of his own pocket in order to free the state from the oppression of a political faction (paragraph 1). He stamped out the civil wars and offered pardons to those who asked for them (paragraph 3). But he does not mention that it was unconstitutional for him as a private citizen to raise an army or that many of his political enemies were executed after he came to power.

Nowhere in the *Res Gestae* does Augustus name any of his political enemies. His rival Antony is obliquely referred to as a participant in factional strife (paragraph 1); his fellow triumvir Lepidus is depicted as an opportunist who usurped the priesthood of the *pontifex maximus* during a period of civil strife (paragraph 10); Sextus Pompeius is the leader of a slave revolt (paragraph 25); the Republicans responsible for the assassination of Julius Caesar are described by the phrase "those who killed my father" (paragraph 2).

Augustus' manipulation of the facts appears prominently in his description of his constitutional powers. In the penultimate paragraph (34) of the *Res Gestae* he proudly relates that he restored the Republic after years of civil war, but what he does not tell the reader is that he received from the Senate extraordinary proconsular powers that permitted him to maintain control of all major standing Roman armies and thus for all intents and purposes control of the Roman government. Augustus' disingenuousness extended also to foreign affairs. The *Res Gestae* contains no mention of any of the military debacles or diplomatic failures that occurred during his reign. And one particulary successful diplomatic venture, namely the one by which the Parthian king Phrates IV was induced to return captured Roman legionary standards, is presented as if it were instead a military campaign (paragraph 29).

The *Res Gestae* cannot be read then as a simple description of the important events in the political, military, and diplomatic career of Augustus. There is the truth, and then there is Augustus' version of it. And Augustus' version must be measured, inasmuch as this is possible, against the historical record that can be established from other contemporary or near-contemporary sources (Suetonius, Tacitus, Cassius Dio, Velleius Paterculus, Plutarch). Of course this is what makes the *Res Gestae* so much more interesting than a mere summation of Augustus' public achievements.

§2. Orthography & Grammar

§2.1 Orthography

There are several features of orthography employed on the *Monumentum Ancyranum* and the *Monumentum Antiochenum* that may present difficulties for readers. They are described in the following sections.

Double Consonants

Double consonants are regularly spelled. There are, however, several words in which both -ss- and -s- are found, e.g. **caussa** and **causa**, **claussum** and **clausum**. This variation reflects a change in pronunciation from double to single -s- after long vowels and diphthongs that was in progress during this period.

Etymological Spellings

A handful of words show vacillation between forms with assimilation and forms with "etymological" spellings, e.g., numquam vs. nunquam, conlēga vs. collēga, and conlēgia vs. collēgia.

Long Vowels

In the Latin versions of the *Res Gestae* the long vowels ā, ē, ō, and ū were indicated—though by no means consistently—by apices (á) written over the vowel. For the long vowel -ī, however, the engravers employed the convention of making the vertical stroke of the i extend beyond the height of other letters in the line, so-called I-*longa*. On a few occasions long ī is spelled by the digraph **ei**, e.g., **Dalmateis** abl. pl. = **Dalmatīs**, **quadrīgeis** abl. pl. = **quadrīgīs**, **ēmeriteis** abl. pl. = **ēmeritīs**. In this text the spelling **ei** for ī is maintained, and words with this spelling feature are listed in the notes.

Medial u vs. i

The spelling of the short vowel in open medial syllables before labial consonants (**p**, **b**, **m**) varied between **u** and **i** in Classical Latin, e.g., **optumus** vs. **optimus**, **maxumus** vs. **maximus**, etc. Although **i** is the letter of choice from the period of Caesar on, there are a handful of words in which the spelling with **u** is codified as the norm, e.g., **documentum**. Examples of words with spellings different from that commonly attested in Classical Latin are **manibiae, reciperō, septuāgēnsumum**, etc., cf. Classical Latin **manubiae, recuperō, septuāgēnsimum**.

§2.2 Declension

The forms of nouns, pronouns, and adjectives require little special commentary. Peculiar aspects of word-forms are discussed as they arise in the text. However, some general features of inflection, particularly those that are not always appropriately described in introductory texts, are noted here.

is, ea, id

The pronominal forms **is, ea, id** have a dative/ablative plural built from a stem in **i-**, giving **iīs**. Other case forms, except for the irregular genitive singular **eius**, have a stem **e-**, for example, **eum, eam, eō, eā, ea, eōrum, eōs**.

2nd Declension Genitive Singular

The genitive singular of 2nd declension nouns with a nominative singular in -ius or -ium is -ī, e.g. congiārī, Feretrī, Iūlī, corōnārī, proelī. This is the regular ending for this declensional type. Genitives in -iī, of which there is one example in this inscription (conlēgiī), are secondary formations with stem final -i introduced into the genitive from other case forms, e.g., conlēgiō, etc.

1st and 2nd Declension Dative/Ablative Plural

The dative / ablative plural of 1st and 2nd declension nouns with nominative singulars in -ia and -ius or -ium varies between -iīs (cōnsiliīs, manibiīs, mūnicipiīs, victōriīs) and -īs (stīpendīs, praemīs, prōvincīs, mūnicipīs, colōnīs, auspicīs, quadrīgīs), the latter being a contraction of original -iīs.

2nd Declension Genitive Plural

The 2nd declension nouns deus, nummus, and sēstertius have a genitive plural ending -um, e.g., deum, nummum, sēstertium.

The Ablative Plural of deus

The ablative plural of deus regularly appears in the *Res Gestae* as dīs, not deīs. Dīs is the form expected on etymological grounds. Deīs, which is commonly found in introductory texts, is a post-Augustan formation.

3rd Declension i-stems and Consonant-stems

I-stem adjectives and nouns regularly have an ablative singular in -ī (marī, cōnsulārī, servīlī, penetrālī). I-stem accusative plurals vary, sometimes -īs, e.g., curūlīs, sometimes -ēs, e.g., Vestālēs, saeclārēs. The adjective omnis has both omnīs and omnēs for the accusative plural.

Consonant-stems regularly have an ablative singular in -e (auctōre, valētūdine, dēferente, occāsiōne, cōnfluente, multitūdine, cōnsule, urbe, prīncipe), but the adjective praesēns has -ī (praesentī abl. sg.). Accusative plurals are generally -ēs (cōnsulēs, sacerdōtēs, pontificēs, virginēs), but -īs is attested in the adjective plūrīs. Present participles have accusative plurals in both -īs and -ēs, e.g., īnferentīs, agentīs, but labentēs. The regular consonant-stem genitive plural ending -um appears in **sacerdōtum**, **hominum**, etc., but one noun, **cīvitās**, stem **cīvitāt**-, has the i-stem genitive plural ending -ium, **cīvitātium**.

§2.3 Conjugation

With the exception of the forms discussed below, the verbs in the *Res Gestae* do not require special comment.

eō "to go"

Compounds of the verb **eō** "to go" have 3rd singular indicative perfects ending in -īt, e.g., **adīt** "approached," and 1st singular forms ending in -ī, e.g., **redī** "returned," both of which are the result of the contraction of **-ii-** or **-iī**. Compare the dative/ablative plural forms cited above, §2.2.

fuēre

The 3rd plural perfect active ending **-ērunt** is found in all of the perfect forms in the *Res Gestae*, except for a single instance of **-ēre**, which appears in the perfect of the verb "to be," **fuēre**. It is not clear why this form of the 3rd plural perfect ending is found only in this verb. During the classical period both endings are attested; **-ēre** is more common in poetry.

The Perfect Passive Infinitive

In the *Res Gestae* the formation of the perfect passive infinitive is occasionally constructed from the perfect participle plus the perfect infinitive **fuisse**, e.g., **clausum fuisse** (paragraph 13), rather than the present infinitive **esse**. Functionally, the two constructions appear to be the same.

§2.4 Syntax

The syntax of the *Res Gestae* is reasonably straightforward and in general should cause little difficulty. A handful of subordinate clause constructions, which are potentially troublesome, are commented on *ad loc.* and so will not be discussed here. The syntax of numerals, which plays a prominent role in paragraphs 15 and following, is also discussed *ad loc.*

Word Order in Subordinate clauses

One feature of the *Res Gestae*, and of classical Latin prose in general, that deserves a brief comment is the placement of important phrases in front of the subordinate clause they belong to, usually in sentence-initial position. There are several examples of this word-order in the text, and all are discussed in the notes. I provide one example here, selected from paragraph 10.

Pontifex maximus nē fierem in vīvī conlēgae meī locum, populō id sacerdōtium dēferente mihi quod pater meus habuerat, recūsāvī.

In the sentence cited above, the object clause, governed by **recūsāvī**, is introduced by the conjunction **nē**. **Pontifex maximus** is positioned outside of its subordinate clause even though it is a predicative noun phrase depending on the verb **fierem**. This word-order strategy is employed as a way of highlighting important information.

"Connective" Relative

Another common feature of the *Res Gestae* and of classical Latin prose is the use of relative pronouns and adjectives to connect clauses that are syntactically independent. In this function the relative words do not introduce subordinate clauses, rather they are the functional equivalent of a third person pronoun or a demonstrative. The following example from paragraph 23, line 4, illustrates this usage.

Nāvālis proelī spectāclum populō dedī trāns Tiberim, in quō locō nunc nemus est Caesarum, cavātō solō in longitūdinem mīlle et octingentōs pedēs, in lātitūdinem mīlle et ducentī. In quō trīgintā rōstrātae nāvēs trirēmēs aut birēmēs, plūrēs autem minōrēs inter sē cōnflīxērunt.

In the second sentence the relative pronoun **quō** functions as a demonstrative, and refers back to the noun **spectāclum** in the preceding sentence. Translate, "In this (show) . . . "

§3. Features of the text

Vocabulary entries, grammatical notes, and historical commentary are combined together on the pages facing the text of the inscription.

The notes and commentary are keyed to words and phrases in the text and are formally set off from the vocabulary entries by the use of a colon placed after the keywords. Words not found in the running list of vocabulary on the pages facing the text are given in the vocabulary list at the end of the book.

The *Res Gestae* contains many references to provincial territories and foreign lands, as well as to many important landmarks in the city of Rome. A map of the Roman Empire, a map of Rome, and a map of the area of the Roman Forum (Figs. 6, 7, 8) are provided so that these references may be located. An index of the names and places mentioned in the *Res Gestae* is also provided.

§4. Bibliography

Bibliographic sources for the *Res Gestae*, Augustus, and the Augustan Age are legion. The books listed here are intended to serve as guideposts for exploring the vast literature on these topics.

Res Gestae

Brunt, Paul, A. and John Michael Moore. 1967. *Res Gestae Divi Augusti. The Achievement of the Divine Augustus.* Oxford: Oxford University Press.

Ehrenberg, Victor, and Arnold Hugh Martin Jones. 1976, reprint of 2nd ed. *Documents Illustrating the Reigns of Augustus and Tiberius.* Oxford: Oxford University Press.

Gagé, Jean. 1977, reprint of 3rd ed. *Res gestae divi Augusti ex monumentis Ancyrano et Antiocheno latinis Ancyrano et Apolloniensi Graecis.* Paris: Société d'édition des belles lettres.

Robinson, David M. 1926. "The *Res Gestae Divi Augusti,* as Recorded on the *Monumentum Antiochenum.*" *American Journal of Philology* 47.1–54.

Volkmann, Hans. 1969, 3rd ed. *Res gestae divi Augusti. Das Monumentum Ancyranum.* Berlin: de Gruyter.

Augustus and His Age

Bowman, Alan K., Edward Champlin, and Andrew Linott (eds.). 1982, 2nd ed. *The Cambridge Ancient History. Vol. X. The Augustan Empire, 43 B.C.–A.D. 69.* Cambridge: Cambridge University Press.

Brunt, Paul A. 1988. *The Fall of the Roman Empire and related essays.* Oxford: Clarendon Press.

Holmes, Thomas Rice. 1928–1931. *The Architect of the Roman Empire. Vol. 1: 44–27 BC; Vol. 2: 27 BC to AD 14*. Oxford: Clarendon Press.

Jones, Arnold Hugh Martin. 1977, reprint of 1st ed. *Augustus*. New York: Norton.

Rowell, Henry Thompson. 1962. *Rome in the Augustan Age*. Norman: University of Oklahoma Press.

Shotter, David Colin Arthur. 1991. *Augustus Caesar*. London and New York: Routledge.

Shuckburgh, Evelyn Shirley. 1903. *Augustus: The Life and Times of the Founder of the Roman Empire*. London: T. F. Unwin.

Southern, Pat. 1998. *Augustus*. London and New York: Routledge.

Syme, Ronald. 1939. *The Roman Revolution*. Oxford: Oxford University Press.

Wallace–Hadrill, Andrew. 1993. *Augustan Rome*. London: Bristol Classical Press.

Architecture, Art, Literature

Galinsky, Karl. 1996. *Augustan Culture. An Interpretative Introduction*. Princeton, NJ: Princeton University Press.

Powel, Anton (ed.). 1992. *Roman Poetry and Propaganda in the Age of Augustus*. London: Bristol Classical Press.

Woodman, Antony, and David West (eds.). 1984. *Poetry and Politics in the Age of Augustus*. Cambridge: Cambridge University Press.

Zanker, Paul (translated by Paul Shapiro). 1988. *The Power of Images in the Age of Augustus*. Ann Arbor: The University of Michigan Press.

RES GESTAE DIVI AUGUSTI

Grammatical Notes
Historical Commentary
Facing Vocabulary

Preamble

1 **gerō, gerere, gessī, gestum**, *to carry, wear; bear; administer, conduct, manage.*

rēs gestae, rērum gestārum, f. pl., *accomplishments.*

Rērum gestārum . . . et impēnsārum . . . incīsārum . . . exemplar subiectum [est]: *a copy of . . . has been placed below.* The genitives **Rērum gestārum** and **impēnsārum** are governed by **exemplar.** The past participle **incīsārum** modifies **Rērum gestārum** and **impēnsārum.**

dīvus, -a, -um, *deified.*

Augustus, -ī , m., *Augustus.* This is the name that was bestowed upon Octavian by the Senate in 27 B.C. (see paragraph 34, line 5). He was born **Gāius Octāvius**, but changed his name to **Gāius Iūlius dīvī fīlius Caesar Octāviānus** after his adoption by Julius Caesar.

2 **subiciō, subicere, subiēcī, subiectum**, *to place underneath/below;* + dat., *to make subject to.*

impēnsa, -ae, f., *expense.*

impēnsam facere: *to incur an expense.*

3 **incīdō, incīdere, incīsī, incīsum**, *to engrave, inscribe.*

4 **ahēneus, -a, -um**, *made of bronze.*

pīla, -ae, f., *pillar* (erected as a monument).

Rōmae: locative, *at Rome.*

exemplar, exemplāris, n., *copy.* The *Monumentum Ancyranum* and the *Monumentum Antiochenum* are copies of the inscription that Augustus set up in front of his Mausoleum in Rome. The introductory section of the original may have ended with the verb **fēcit**. See INTRODUCTION §1.2 for discussion of the preamble.

subiectum: supply **est**, *has been placed below.*

1 Rērum gestārum dīvī Augustī, quibus orbem terrārum

2 imperiō populī Rōmānī subiēcit, et impēnsārum, quās in rem

3 pūblicam populumque Rōmānum fēcit, incīsārum in duābus

4 ahēneīs pīlīs, quae sunt Rōmae positae, exemplar subiectum.

1

1 **Annōs undēvīgintī nātus**: *At nineteen years of age.* A person's age is
expressed by the past participle of the verb **nāscor, nāscī, nātus,** *to be
born,* with an accusative of duration of time. Octavian was nineteen
on September 23, 44 B.C.

exercitum . . . comparāvī: Octavian could not legally raise an army as a
private citizen. His actions were sanctioned after the fact by the
Senate in January, 43 B.C. (See below, lines 4–8.)

prīvātus, -a, -um, *one's own, private.*

3 **dominātiō, dominātiōnis,** f., *tyranny, power.*

ā dominātiōne: ablative of agent with **oppressum.** This construction is
used with names of things or qualities when they are conceived of as
personified.

factiōnis: the reference is to Mark Antony. In this inscription Augustus
does not mention the names of his enemies.

vindicō, -āre, -āvī, -ātum, *to deliver, free, liberate.*

in libertātem vindicāre: *to free from oppressive rule, liberate.*

Eō nōmine: *For this reason.*

4 **dēcrētum, -ī,** n., *decree.*

honōrificus, -a, -um, *bestowing honor.*

dēcrētīs honōrificīs: Augustus refers to proposals by Cicero and Publius
Servilius that were adopted by the Senate on January 1, 43 B.C. By
the terms of these proposals, Octavian was declared senator with the
rank of propraetor and was given the right to express his opinion
with the consuls. The order of speaking in the Senate was deter-
mined by the magistracies a senator had held.

ōrdō, ōrdinis, m., *order, rank, class.*

5 **adlegō, adlegere, adlēgī, adlēctum,** *to appoint, elect.*

C. Pānsā et A. Hirtiō: Gaius Pansa and Aulus Hirtius, consuls in 43 B.C.

locus, -ī, m., *rank, position, precedence.*

6 **sententia, -ae,** f., *opinion.*

sententiae dīcendae: a gerundive phrase in the dative case generally
signals purpose, *for the purpose of speaking my opinion.* Compare the
gerundive phrase **reī pūblicae cōnstituendae** in line 10.

tribuō, tribuere, tribuī, tribūtum, *to award, grant, bestow.*

imperium: Octavian was given the **imperium** of a praetor and thus the
right to hold a military command.

7 **dētrīmentum, -ī,** n., *harm, damage.*

Rēs pūblica nē quid dētrīmentī caperet: the subject of the verb **caperet**
is positioned before the conjunction **nē.** The indefinite pronoun
quid is to be taken with the genitive **dētrīmentī** in a partitive construction. The indirect command is governed by the infinitive
prōvidēre. This is the standard senatorial declaration of martial law.

1 §1 Annōs undēvīgintī nātus exercitum prīvātō cōnsiliō et

2 prīvātā impēnsā comparāvī, per quem rem pūblicam ā

3 dominātiōne factiōnis oppressam in lībertātem vindicāvī. Eō

4 nōmine senātus dēcrētīs honōrificīs in ōrdinem suum mē

5 adlēgit, C. Pānsā et A. Hirtiō cōnsulibus, cōnsulārem locum

6 sententiae dīcendae tribuēns, et imperium mihi dedit. Rēs

7 pūblica nē quid dētrīmentī caperet, mē prō praetōre simul cum

8 cōnsulibus prōvidēre iussit. Populus autem eōdem annō

9 mē cōnsulem, cum cōs. uterque in bellō cecidisset, et

10 triumvirum reī pūblicae cōnstituendae creāvit.

---

prō praetōre, indecl. phrase, *propraetor*. The phrase usually refers to ex-
praetors that have been given *imperium* in the provinces for military
or administrative purposes. Octavian received this power by decree
of the Senate.

mē prō praetōre: accusative object of **iussit**.

8 **prōvideō, prōvidēre, prōvīdī, prōvīsum** + **ut/nē** + subjunctive, *to see to it
(that/that . . . not)*.

iussit: the subject is **senātus**. The Senate ordered Octavian and the
consuls Hirtius and Pansa to make war on Antony.

9 **mē cōnsulem . . . creāvit**: *elected me consul*. After the deaths of the
consuls Hirtius and Pansa, Octavian and his cousin Quintus Pedius
were elected as consuls in a special election held in August, 43 B.C.

cōs.: abbreviation for **cōnsul**.

cecidisset: Hirtius and Pansa both died fighting Antony in Cisalpine
Gaul in April, 43 B.C. Pansa was gravely injured at Forum Gallorum
on April 15. He died several days later. Hirtius was killed in a battle
fought near Mutina on April 21.

10 **triumvir, -ī**, m., *triumvir*.

triumvirum: the *lex Titia* granted Octavian, Antony, and Lepidus su-
preme power for the next five years, to January 1, 38 B.C.

reī pūblicae cōnstituendae: dative of purpose.

2

1 Quī: the antecedent of the relative pronoun is eōs. The reference is to the
    assassins of Julius Caesar.
   parentem meum: Octavian was Julius Caesar's adopted son.
   trucīdō, -āre, -āvī, -ātum, *to butcher, massacre, slaughter.*
   exilium, -ī, n., *exile.*
2 iūdicium, -ī, n., *legal proceedings.*
   lēgitimus, -a, -um, *lawful.*
   iūdiciīs lēgitimīs: those implicated in Julius Caesar's death were con-
    demned by a law (the *lex Pedia*) sponsered by the consul Quintus
    Pedius in August or September, 43 B.C.
   ulcīscor, ulcīscī, ultus, *to avenge, punish.*
   ultus: the perfect participle of deponent verbs is active in voice and is
    often translated with a present tense in English.
   facinus, facinoris, n., *crime.*
3 īnferentīs: acc. pl., modifying eōs. The participle governs the accusative
    bellum (as direct object) and the dative reī pūblicae (after com-
    pound verbs), *waging war against the state.*
   bis: Augustus refers to the two battles against Brutus and Cassius at
    Philippi, Macedonia, in October and November of 42 B.C. Because
    Octavian was bedridden with an illness, Antony was largely respon-
    sible for both victories.
   aciēs, aciēī, f., *battle.*

3

1 terrā et marī: a preposition is not required with the ablative to indicate
    place where.
   cīvīlis, -is, -e, *occurring between citizens, civil.*
   externus, -a, -um, *foreign.*
3 tūtō, adv., *safely, securely.*
   ignōscō, ignōscere, ignōvī, ignōtum + dat., *to pardon, forgive.*
   quibus tūtō ignōscī potuit: the subject of potuit is the infinitive ignōscī,
    which is itself an impersonal passive governing the relative pronoun
    quibus. Translate, *to whom pardon could be securely given.*
4 cōnservō, -āre, -āvī, -ātum, *to preserve.*
   excīdō, excīdere, excīdī, excīsum, *to destroy, exterminate.*
   mīllia (= mīlia): modified by quīngenta.
5 sacrāmentum, -ī, n., *military oath of allegiance.*
   sub sacrāmentō meō: in 33 B.C. the cities of Italy and the provinicials in
    Gaul, Spain, Africa, and Sicily swore an oath of loyalty to Octavian.
   circiter, adv., *approximately, roughly.*
6 colōnia, -ae, f., *colony, settlement.*
   mūnicipium, -ī, n., *community, municipality, town.*
   stīpendium, -ī, n., *military service.*

1 §2 Quī parentem meum trucīdāvērunt, eōs in exilium expulī
2 iūdiciīs lēgitimīs ultus eōrum facinus et posteā bellum
3 īnferentīs reī pūblicae vīcī bis aciē.

1 §3 Bella terrā et marī cīvīlia externaque tōtō in orbe terrārum
2 saepe gessī, victorque omnibus veniam petentibus cīvibus
3 pepercī. Externās gentēs, quibus tūtō ignōscī potuit,
4 cōnservāre quam excīdere māluī. Mīllia cīvium Rōmānōrum
5 sub sacrāmentō meō fuērunt circiter quīngenta. Ex quibus
6 dēdūxī in colōniās aut remīsī in mūnicipia sua stīpendīs
7 ēmeritīs mīllia aliquantō plūra quam trecenta, et iīs omnibus
8 agrōs adsignāvī aut pecūniam prō praemīs mīlitiae dedī.
9 Nāvēs cēpī sescentās praeter eās, sī quae minōrēs quam
10 trirēmēs fuērunt.

---

stīpendīs: the final vowel -i of the stem (stīpendi-) and the -ī of the
  ablative plural ending -īs have contracted. See INTRODUCTION §2.2.
7 ēmereō, -ēre, -uī, -itum, *to serve out, complete.*
  stīpendīs ēmeritīs: ablative absolute, *after (their) military service had been
    served out.*
  aliquantō, adv., *to some extent, by a considerable amount.*
  trecentī, -ae, -a, *three hundred.*
  iīs: dative plural of is, ea, id.
8 adsignō, -āre, -āvī, -ātum, *to assign.*
  prō: = *as.*
  praemium, -ī, n., *reward, recompense.*
  praemīs: = praemiīs. See note on stīpendīs, line 6.
  mīlitia, -ae, f., *military service.*
9 Nāvēs: ships captured from Sextus Pompeius in 36 B.C. and from Antony
    and Cleopatra in 31 B.C.
  sescentī, -ae, -a, *six hundred.*
  quis, qua/quae, quid, indef. adj., *some, any.*
  quae: feminine, nominative, plural modifying an understood nāvēs.
10 trirēmis, trirēmis, f., *trireme (ship with three banks of oars).*

4

1 **ovō, -āre, -āvī, -ātum**, *to celebrate an ovation*. An ovation was a lesser form of a triumph (see below, **triumphō**). In an ovation, the victorious Roman general paraded through the city of Rome on foot or on horseback.

bis ovāns: Octavian celebrated one ovation with Antony after the treaty of Brundisium in 40 B.C. The second ovation was in November, 36 B.C., after victories over Sextus Pompeius in Sicily.

triumphō, -āre, -āvī, -ātum, *to celebrate a triumph*. The word is used here of the lesser form of triumph, the ovation.

trēs, trēs, tria, *three*.

trīs: acc. pl., modifying **triumphōs**.

curūlis, -is, -e, *curule*. The adjective *curule* referred originally to a chair with ivory inlay that was used by the chief magistrates of the Roman state.

curūlīs: acc. pl., modifying **triumphōs**. A curule triumph involved a magnificent procession in which the victorious general rode in a four-horse chariot. He was accompanied in the parade by Roman magistrates and Roman senators. The parade started near the Campus Martius, circled the Palatine Hill, and finished at the Temple of Jupiter on the Capitoline Hill.

triumphus, -ī, m., *triumphal procession*.

triumphōs: for the campaigns in Illyricum (34–33 B.C.), for the defeat of Antony and Cleopatra at Actium (31 B.C.), and for the capture of Egypt (30 B.C.). The triumphs were celebrated on three consecutive days (13, 14, 15) in August, 29 B.C.

2 **vīciēns**, adv., *twenty times*.

semel, adv., *once, one time*.

imperātor: a victorious general was hailed by his troops as **imperātor**.

dēcernō, dēcernere, dēcrēvī, dēcrētum, *to decree*.

plūrīs: acc. pl., modifying **triumphōs**.

3 **supersedeō, supersedēre, supersēdī, supersessum** + dat. or abl., *to abstain from; to pass over*.

Laurum: a victorious general, hailed as **imperator**, wreathed the **fascēs** with bay leaves.

4 **Capitōlium, -ī**, n., *Capitol, Capitoline Hill*. It was customary for a victorious general to deposit the bay wreath on the Capitol when he returned to Rome after a military campaign.

vōtum, -ī, n., *vow, promise*.

quisque, quaeque, quodque, adj., *every, each*.

5 **nuncupō, -āre, -āvī, -ātum**, *to utter, pronounce*.

rēs: = *campaigns*.

6 **auspicium, -ī**, n., *leadership, authority*; pl., *auspices*.

auspicīs meīs: ablative of attendant circumstances.

1 §4 Bis ovāns triumphāvī et trīs ēgī curūlīs triumphōs, et

2 appellātus sum vīciēns et semel imperātor, dēcernente plūrīs

3 triumphōs mihi senātū quibus omnibus supersēdī. Laurum dē

4 fascibus dēposuī in Capitōliō, vōtīs quae quōque bellō

5 nuncupāveram solūtīs. Ob rēs ā mē aut per lēgātōs meōs

6 auspicīs meīs terrā marīque prosperē gestās quīnquāgiēns et

7 quīnquiēns dēcrēvit senātus supplicandum esse dīs

8 immortālibus. Diēs autem, per quōs ex senātūs cōnsultō

9 supplicātum est, fuēre DCCCLXXXX. In triumphīs meīs ductī

10 sunt ante currum meum rēgēs aut rēgum līberī novem. Consul

11 fueram terdeciēns, cum scrībēbam haec, et eram septimum et

12 trīcēnsimum tribūniciae potestātis.

---

6 **prosperē**, adv., *successfully.*
  quīnquāgiēns, adv., *fifty times.*
7 **quīnquiēns**, adv., *five times.*
  supplicō, -āre, -āvī, -ātum + dat., *to worship; to make thank offerings to.*
  supplicandum esse dīs immortālibus: indirect statement governed by
      dēcrēvit. supplicandum esse: this construction is impersonal.
  dīs: dative plural of **deus, -ī.**
9 **supplicātum est**: impersonal passive of the intransitive verb.
  ex: *in accordance with.*
  fuēre: = **fuērunt.**
10 **currus, -ūs**, m., *chariot.*
  rēgēs aut rēgum līberī: most notably the children of Antony and
      Cleopatra.
11 **terdeciēns**, adv., *thirteen times.* Augustus was consul in 43, 33, 31–23, 5,
      and 2 B.C.
  septimum, adv., *for the seventh time.*
12 **trīcēnsimum**, adv., *for the thirtieth time.*
  tribūnicius, -a, -um, *tribunician.*
  tribūniciae potestātis: genitive of description; translate *a man of. . . .*
      Tribunician power gave Augustus the right to submit legislation to
      the citizen assemblies, the right to convene the Senate and to make
      motions in that body, and the right of veto over other magistrates.

5

1 **dictātūra, -ae**, f., *dictatorship.*
   dictātūram: the dictatorship was offered to Augustus so that he could relieve a severe grain shortage plaguing Rome. He refused the office in 22 B.C.
   apsēns, apsentis, *absent.*
   praesēns, praesentis, *present.*
2 **M. Marcellō et L. Arruntiō**: Marcus Marcellus and Lucius Arruntius, consuls in 22 B.C.
3 **dēprecor, -ārī, -ātus**, *to refuse, decline.*
   frūmentum, -ī, n., *corn, grain.*
   pēnūria, -ae, f., *shortage, scarcity.*
   cūrātiō, cūrātiōnis, f., *superintendence, administration.*
4 **annōna, -ae**, f., *grain-supply.*
   administrō, -āre, -āvī, -ātum, *to administer.*
5 **perīclō**: = **perīculō.**
   praesentī: abl. sg., modifying **perīclō**; translate *immediate.*
   cīvitās, cīvitātis, f., *city, town.*
6 **cōnsulātus, -ūs**, m., *consulship.*
   tum: 22 B.C.
   annuus, -a, -um, *annual.*
   annuum et perpetuum: automatically renewed every year by election.

6

1 **M. Viniciō et Q. Lucrētiō**: Marcus Vinicius and Quintus Lucretius, consuls in 19 B.C.
   P. Lentulō et Cn. Lentulō: Publius Lentulus and Gnaeus Lentulus, consuls in 18 B.C.
2 **tertium**, adv., *for a third time.*
   Paullō Fabiō Maximō et Q. Tuberōne: Paullus Fabius Maximus and Quintus Tubero, consuls in 11 B.C.
3 **cōnsentiō, cōnsentīre, cōnsēnsī, cōnsēnsum**, *to agree.*
   senātū et populōque Rōmānō cōnsentientibus: ablative absolute, *when/ although.* . . .
   ut . . . creārer: indirect command governed by the participle **cōnsentientibus.**
   cūrātor, cūrātōris, m., *supervisor, superintendent, curator.*
   lēx, lēgis, f., *law.*
4 **mōs, mōris**, m., *custom, usage, fashion*; pl., *conduct, behavior, morals, character.*
   summā potestāte: ablative of manner, *with.* . . .
   sōlus: i.e., without a colleague.
   magistrātus, -ūs, m., *magistracy.*

1 §5 Dictātūram et apsentī et praesentī mihi dēlātam et ā populō
2 et ā senātū M. Marcellō et L. Arruntiō cōnsulibus nōn recēpī.
3 Nōn sum dēprecātus in summā frūmentī pēnūriā cūrātiōnem
4 annōnae, quam ita administrāvī, ut intrā diēs paucōs metū et
5 perīclō praesentī cīvitātem ūniversam līberārem impēnsā et cūrā
6 meā. Cōnsulātum quoque tum annuum et perpetuum mihi
7 dēlātum nōn recēpī.

1 §6 Cōnsulibus M. Vinīciō et Q. Lucrētiō et posteā P. Lentulō et
2 Cn. Lentulō et tertium Paullō Fabiō Maximō et Q. Tuberōne
3 senātū populōque Rōmānō cōnsentientibus ut cūrātor lēgum et
4 mōrum summā potestāte sōlus creārer, nūllum magistrātum
5 contrā mōrem maiōrum dēlātum recēpī. Quae tum per mē gerī
6 senātus voluit, per tribūniciam potestātem perfēcī, cuius
7 potestātis conlēgam et ipse ultrō quīnquiēns ā senātū dēpoposcī
8 et accēpī.

---

cūrātor . . . nūllum magistrātum: supervision of morals was a regular
    part of the duty of a censor.
5 Quae: *And those things that.* The antecedent is omitted. This phrase
    refers to the things the Senate wanted Augustus to do as cūrātor
    lēgum et mōrum. In 18 B.C. Augustus enacted legislation encourag-
    ing marriage among members of the upper classes and punishing
    adultery.
6 conlēga, -ae, m., *partner, colleague.*
    conlēga: preserving the etymological spelling; compare the spelling
        collēga in which -n is assimilated to -l.
    ultrō, adv., *on one's own initiative, of one's own accord.*
    quīnquiēns: tribunician power was granted to Agrippa in 18 B.C. and 13
        B.C., and to Tiberius in 6 B.C., A.D. 4, and A.D. 13.
    dēposcō, dēposcere, dēpoposcī, *to demand.*

7

1   **triumvirum**: = **triumvirōrum**, gen. pl.; partitive genitive, *a member of the board of three men; i.e., a member of the triumvirate.*

reī pūblicae cōnstituendae: dative of purpose. For this gerundive construction see paragraph 1, line 6.

continuus, -a, -um, *successive, consecutive.*

per continuōs annōs decem: Augustus was **triumvir** for two five-year terms from 43 to 33 B.C.

2   **prīnceps senātūs**: this is the title given to the preeminent man in the Senate.

usque ad + acc., *right up to.*

3   **scrīpseram**: this is an "epistolary" pluperfect, which is best translated as a simple past in English.

pontifex, pontificis, m., *Roman high-priest.*

pontifex maximus: *chief priest* (head of the college of **pontificēs**, the priestly college in control of public religion in Rome). Augustus assumed this priestly office in 12 B.C. See also paragraph 10, lines 4–10.

4   **augur, auguris**, m., *augur, diviner.*

quīndecimvirum: gen. pl.; partitive genitive, *a member of the college of fifteen men/priests.* The **quindecimvirī** were in charge of the Sibylline books and the ceremonies prescribed in them.

sacrīs faciundīs: dative of purpose. Compare with the construction in line 1. The gerundive **faciundīs** has the suffix -**und**- instead of the more common -**end**-, cf. **dīcendae**, paragraph 1, line 6.

septemvirum epulōnum: *a member of the college of seven men/priests.* The **septemvirī** were responsible for arranging public feasts in honor of the gods.

5   **epulō, epulōnis**, m., *banqueter, diner.*

frāter arvālis: *arval brother* (member of the college of twelve priests who made annual offerings to the *Dea Dia* for a bountiful harvest).

sodālis, sodālis, m., *member of a society/fraternity/priesthood.*

Titius: the title of an obscure priesthood.

fētiālis, fētiālis, m., *fetial priest* (one of the college of priests who represented the Roman People in making peace treaties and declaring war).

1 §7 Triumvirum reī pūblicae cōnstituendae fuī per continuōs
2 annōs decem. Prīnceps senātūs fuī usque ad eum diem quō
3 scrīpseram haec per annōs quadrāgintā. Pontifex māximus,
4 augur, quīndecimvirum sacrīs faciundīs, septemvirum
5 epulōnum, frāter arvālis, sodālis Titius, fētiālis fuī.

8

1   **patriciī, -ōrum**, m. pl., *patricians, nobility.*

     patriciōrum: Octavian added members to the old Roman aristocracy, the so-called patricians, because their numbers had been depleted in the civil wars.

     quīntum, adv., *for the fifth time.*

     cōnsul quīntum: 29 B.C.

     iussus, -ūs, m., *order.*

2   **legō, legere, lēgī, lēctum**, *to choose, select, pick;* here, *to revise the membership of.*

     senātum ter lēgī: Augustus eliminated members whom he considered to be unqualified.

     in cōnsulātū sextō: 28 B.C.

     cēnsus, -ūs, m., *registration of Roman citizens, census.*

     conlēgā M. Agrippā: ablative absolute. Marcus Agrippa was the life-long friend and trusted companion of Augustus. He married Augustus' only daughter, Julia, in 23 B.C. after the death of her first husband, Marcellus.

     lūstrum, -ī, n., *lustration, ceremony of purification.* It was customary for a lustration to be performed after the census had been taken.

     alter, altera, alterum, here, *second.* This meaning is common when **alter** is used in a numerical or temporal series.

4   **quadrāgēnsimus, -a, -um**, *fortieth.*

     post annum alterum et quadrāgēnsium: = 42 years after the previous census had been taken. The Romans counted back from the original year of the previous census, which was in 70 B.C.

     Quō lūstrō: the term **lūstrum** is used here and below in lines 7 and 11 as an equivalent of the term **cēnsus**.

     cēnseō, cēnsēre, cēnsuī, cēnsum, *to register/enrol* (at a census).

5   **quadrāgiēns**, adv., *forty times.*

     sexāgintā, *sixty.*

     quadrāgiēns centum mīllia et sexāgintā tria mīllia: numbers in the millions and higher were expressed by **mīllia** plus numerical adverbs. Thus, the number is 40 x 100,000 (**centum mīllia**) plus 63,000 = 4,063,000.

6   **C. Cēnsōrīnō et C. Asiniō cōs.**: Gaius Censorinus and Gaius Asinius, consuls in 8 B.C.

     cōs.: abbreviation for **cōnsulibus**.

     iterum: *a second time.*

8   **ducentī, -ae, -a**, *two hundred.*

9   **trīgintā**, *thirty.*

10   **Tib.**: abbreviation for Tiberius.

1 §8 Patriciōrum numerum auxī cōnsul quīntum iussū populī et
2 senātūs. Senātum ter lēgī. Et in cōnsulātū sextō cēnsum
3 populī conlēgā M. Agrippā ēgī. Lūstrum post annum alterum
4 et quadrāgēnsimum fēcī. Quō lūstrō cīvium Rōmānōrum cēnsa
5 sunt capita quadrāgiēns centum mīllia et sexāgintā tria mīllia.
6 Tum iterum cōnsulārī cum imperiō lūstrum sōlus fēcī C.
7 Cēnsōrīnō et C. Asiniō cōs. Quō lūstrō cēnsa sunt cīvium
8 Rōmānōrum capita quadrāgiēns centum mīllia et ducenta
9 trīgintā tria mīllia. Et tertium cōnsulārī cum imperiō lūstrum
10 conlēgā Tib. Caesare fīliō meō fēcī Sex. Pompēiō et Sex.
11 Appulēiō cōs. Quō lūstrō cēnsa sunt cīvium Rōmānōrum
12 capitum quadrāgiēns centum mīllia et nōngenta trīgintā et
13 septem mīllia. Lēgibus novīs mē auctōre lātīs multa exempla
14 maiōrum exolēscentia iam ex nostrō saeculō redūxī et ipse
15 multārum rērum exempla imitanda posterīs trādidī.

Sex. Pompēiō et Sex. Appulēiō cōs.: Sextus Pompeius and Sextus
  Appuleius, consuls in A.D. 14.
12 **capitum**: partitive genitive with **mīllia**; compare lines 5 and 8 above
   where **mīllia** is in agreement with **capita**.
   nōngentī, -ae, -a, *nine hundred.*
13 **Lēgibus . . . lātīs**: ablative absolute. The laws referred to here are those
   constituting Augustus' moral, social, and religious reforms. Compare paragraph 6, lines 3–8.
   auctor, auctōris, m., *advocate, supporter; mover, proposer* (of a law).
   ferō, ferre, tulī, lātum, here, *to pass a law.*
   exemplum, -ī, n., *example*; pl., *exemplary practices, models of conduct.*
14 **exolēscō, exolēscere, exolēvī, exolētum,** *to fade away, die out.*
   saeculum, -ī, n., *generation.*
   redūxī: *I revived.*
15 **imitor, -ārī, -ātus,** *to imitate, copy.*
   posterī, -ōrum, m. pl., *posterity, descendants.*
   posterīs: note the placement of **posterīs** between **imitanda** and **trādidī.**
   Posterīs may be taken as a dative of agent with **imitanda** or as an
   indirect object with **trādidī.**

9

1   **valētūdō, valētūdinis**, f., *health.*

    prō valētūdine meā: Augustus suffered from chronic ill-health.

    suscipiō, suscipere, suscēpī, susceptum, *to undertake* (an oath, a vow*).*

    suscipī: present passive infinitive. **Vōta . . . suscipī**: accusative and
       infinitive dependent on **dēcrēvit**. Compare the construction in
       paragraph 4, line 7.

    sacerdōs, sacerdōtis, m., *priest.*

2   **Ex**: *In consequence of, in fulfillment of.*

3   **aliquotiēns**, adv., *several times.*

    amplus, -a, -um, *distinguished, eminent.*

4   **collēgium, -ī**, n., *college, organization.*

    quattuor amplissima collēgia: the four priestly colleges were the
       pontificēs, the **augurēs**, the **quindecimvirī**, and the **septemvirī**. See
       paragraph 7, lines 3–5.

    prīvātim, adv., *in private, personally.*

    etiam: translate *moreover.*

    mūnicipātim, adv., *by municipalities.*

5   **ūnanimiter**, adv., *with one purpose/accord.*

    continenter, adv., *continuously.*

    pulvīnar, pulvīnāris, n., *sacred couch* (a cushioned couch on which
       images of gods were made to recline so that they could partake of a
       sacred banquet).

6   **supplicō, -āre, -āvī, -ātum**, here, *to pray; to make propitiatory offerings.*

1 §9 Vōta prō valētūdine meā suscipī per cōnsulēs et sacerdōtēs

2 quīntō quōque annō senātus dēcrēvit. Ex iīs vōtīs saepe fēcērunt

3 vīvō mē lūdōs aliquotiēns sacerdōtum quattuor amplissima

4 collēgia, aliquotiēns cōnsulēs. Prīvātim etiam et mūnicipātim

5 ūniversī cīvēs ūnanimiter continenter apud omnia pulvīnāria

6 prō valētūdine meā supplicāvērunt.

10

1   **inclūdō, inclūdere, inclūsī, inclūsum,** *to incorporate, insert.*

    saliāris, -is, -e, *of the Salii* (a college of twelve priests dedicated to the service of Mars).

    carmen, carminis, n., *song, hymn.*

    saliāre carmen: *hymn of the Salii.* It was the function of this hymn to insure the safety of Rome during wartime.

2   **sacrōsānctus, -a, -um,** *inviolable.*

    sacrōsānctus . . . ut essem: = **ut sacrōsānctus . . . essem.** Note the position of the predicate adjective phrase outside of the clause to which it belongs.

    in perpetum: *permanently.* **perpetum:** acc. sg. with contraction of **uu,** = **perpetuum.** For another example of contraction of **uu** see the fourth declension genitive plural **exercitum,** paragraph 29, line 3.

    quoad, rel. adv., *for as long as, while.*

3   **tribūnicia potestās:** see paragraph 4, line 12.

    sanciō, sancīre, sānxī, sānctum, *to enact, prescribe by law.*

    ut essem . . . sānctum est: the indirect command **ut essem et . . . esset** is the subject of **sānctum est.**

4   **Pontifex maximus nē fierem:** the predicate nominative phrase stands outside of its clause; cf. **sacrosānctus . . . ut essem** above.

    conlēgae meī: Octavian's colleague, Lepidus, became **pontifex maximus,** a position held for life, after the death of Julius Caesar. Lepidus died in 12 B.C. and Augustus was then elected to this priesthood.

5   **sacerdōtium, -ī,** n., *priesthood.*

    pater meus: Julius Caesar.

6   **recūsō, -āre, -āvī, -ātum,** *to reject* (the proposition / idea that + **nē** + subjunctive).

    nē fierem . . . recūsāvī: *I rejected the idea that I become....*

    Quod sacerdōtium: direct object of **recēpī** (line 9).

    aliquod = aliquot, indecl. adj., *some, several.*

    aliquod: modifying **annōs.**

    eō mortuō: ablative absolute.

7   **quī:** the antecedent is the pronoun **eō** in the ablative absolute.

    mōtus, -ūs, m., *civil disorder, disturbance.*

    occāsiō, occāsiōnis, f., *convenient circumstance, opportunity.*

    cīvīlis mōtūs occāsiōne: Lepidus became **pontifex maximus** during the period of chaos following the death of Julius Caesar.

    occupō, -āre, -āvī, -ātum, *to seize, take possession of.*

    cūnctus, -a, -um, *the whole of, all.*

1 §10 Nōmen meum senātūs cōnsultō inclūsum est in saliāre
2 carmen, et sacrōsānctus in perpetum ut essem et quoad
3 vīverem tribūnicia potestās mihi esset, per lēgem sānctum est.
4 Pontifex maximus nē fierem in vīvī conlēgae meī locum, populō
5 id sacerdōtium dēferente mihi quod pater meus habuerat,
6 recūsāvī. Quod sacerdōtium aliquod post annōs, eō mortuō
7 quī cīvīlis mōtūs occāsiōne occupāverat, cūnctā ex Italiā ad
8 comitia mea cōnfluente multitūdine quanta Rōmae nunquam
9 fertur ante id tempus fuisse, recēpī P. Sulpiciō C. Valgiō
10 cōnsulibus.

---

8 **comitium, -ī**, n., *a place of assembly*; pl., *election*.
cōnfluō, cōnfluere, cōnflūxī, *to meet, gather, assemble*.
cūnctā . . . multitūdine: ablative absolute. **multitūdine**: the antecedent
    of **quanta**.
9 **fertur**: *is said*.
P. Sulpiciō C. Valgiō: Publius Sulpicius and Gaius Valgius, consuls in 12
    B.C.

11

1   **Fortūna Redux**: *Fortuna Redux* (goddess, "who leads one safely back home").
     aedēs, aedis, f., *temple.*
     Honōs, Honōris, m., *Honor* (god of military prowess and virtue).
     Virtūs, Virtūtis, f., *Virtue* (goddess of moral excellence).
2   **portam Capēnam**: *Porta Capena.* This gate is located in the southern part of the city at the beginning of the Appian Way. It was the gate by which Augustus entered the city upon his return.
     prō reditū meō: Augustus was abroad in Sicily, Greece, Asia, and Syria from 22 to 19 B.C. During his absence there were serious public disorders.
3   **Vestālis, -is, -e**, *of/belonging to Vesta.*
     virginēs Vestālēs: *Vestal virgins.*
     anniversārius, -a, -um, *celebrated annually, performed annually, annual.*
     sacrificium, -ī, n., *sacrifice.*
4   **Q. Lucrētiō et M. Viniciō**: Quintus Lucretius and Marcus Vinicius, consuls in 19 B.C.
5   **Syria, -ae**, f., *Syria.*
     Augustālia, Augustālium, n. pl., *Augustalia* (the name given to the day in October on which a festival of games in honor of Augustus was celebrated).

12

1   **Senātūs . . . dēcrētus**: the first sentence of paragraph 12 belongs logically with paragraph 11.
     praetor, praetōris, m., *praetor* (public official in charge of judicial proceedings).
     plēbēs, plēbēī, also **plēbī**, m., *plebeians, people.* The genitive **plēbī** appears most commonly in phrases with the nouns **tribūnus**, **aedilis**, and **scītum**.
2   **tribūnōrum plēbī**: the tribunes of the plebs were elected officials with veto power over other elected officials.
     prīnceps, prīncipis, *leading.*
3   **obviam**, adv. + dat., *so as to meet.*
     Campānia, -ae, f., *Campania.*
     quī honōs: the antecedent **honōs** is incorporated into the relative clause = *an honor that. . . .*
4   **cum . . . redī**: **cum** temporal clause with indicative.
     Hispānia, -ae, f., *Spain.*
     Gallia, -ae, f., *Gaul.*

1 §11 Āram Fortūnae Reducis ante aedēs Honōris et Virtūtis ad
2 portam Capēnam prō reditū meō senātus cōnsacrāvit, in quā
3 pontificēs et virginēs Vestālēs anniversārium sacrificium facere
4 iussit eō diē quō cōnsulibus Q. Lucrētiō et M. Viniciō in urbem
5 ex Syriā redieram, et diem Augustālia ex cognōmine nostrō
6 appellāvit.

1 §12 Senātūs cōnsultō eōdem tempore pars praetōrum et
2 tribūnōrum plēbī cum cōnsule Q. Lucrētiō et prīncipibus virīs
3 obviam mihi missa est in Campāniam, quī honōs ad hoc tempus
4 nēminī praeter mē est dēcrētus. Cum ex Hispāniā Galliāque,
5 rēbus in iīs prōvincīs prosperē gestīs, Rōmam redī, Ti. Nerōne
6 P. Quīntiliō cōnsulibus, āram Pācis Augustae senātus prō
7 reditū meō cōnsacrandam cēnsuit ad campum Mārtium, in quā
8 magistrātūs et sacerdōtēs virginēsque Vestālēs anniversārium
9 sacrificium facere iussit.

---

5 **redī**: = redii.
   Ti. Nerōne P. Quīntiliō: Tiberius Nero and Publius Quintilius, consuls
      in 13 B.C.
6 **āram Pācis Augustae**: *the Altar of Augustan Peace.* The altar was built
      alongside the Via Flaminia. It was formally dedicated in January, 9
      B.C.
   prō reditū meō: Augustus was in Spain and Gaul from 16 to 13 B.C.
7 **cōnsacrandam**: understand **esse**. **cōnsacrandam (esse)**: passive peri-
      phrastic in the accusative and infinitive construction governed by
      cēnsuit.
   campus Mārtius, campī Mārtī, m., *Campus Martius* (an open field on the
      banks of the Tiber River where the Roman people met in the
      Centuriate Assembly).

13

1 **Iānus Quirīnus, -ī, m.,** *Doorway of Janus Quirinus* (a shrine of the god
   Janus in the Forum consisting of an archway with doors at each
   end). When the gates were closed it was considered a sign of
   universal peace.
   Iānum Quirīnum: the subject of **claudendum esse** in line 5.
   claussum: = **clausum**. See INTRODUCTION §2.1.
3 **pariō, parere, peperī, partum,** *to give birth to, bear; to bring forth, produce;*
   to procure, get, obtain.
4 **omnīnō, adv.,** *in every respect, all told, altogether.*
   clausum fuisse: = **clausum esse**. See INTRODUCTION §2.3.
   prōdō, prōdere, prōdidī, prōditum + **memoriae,** *to hand down, record.*
   prodātur memoriae: the subject is the indirect statement clause **prius . . .**
     fuisse.
   ter: Augustus closed the gates to the shrine of Janus in January, 29 B.C. ,
     after the battle of Actium and again in 25 B.C. after the Cantabrian
     war. The date of the third closing is not known.

14

1 **Gāium et Lūcium Caesarēs**: the sons of Julia, Augustus' daughter, and
   Marcus Agrippa; they were adopted by Augustus in 17 B.C. They
   were judged to be able to participate in public life at age 15. Gaius
   was designated for the consulship of A.D. 1, which he held; Lucius
   was designated for the consulship of A.D. 4, but he died in A.D. 2.
2 **caussā**: = **causā**. See note on **claussum**, paragraph 13, line 1.
3 **annum quīntum et decimum agentīs**: during their fifteenth year.
   agentīs: acc. pl.
4 **dēsignō, -āre, -āvī, -ātum,** *to appoint, select.*
   quīnquennium, -ī, n., *a period of five years.*
5 **intersum, interesse, interfuī** + dat., *to take part in.*
6 **eques, equitis, m.,** *knight* (social class with minimum property qualification of 400,000 sesterces).
7 **iuventūs, iuventūtis, f.,** *youth.*
   prīncipem iuventūtis: an honorary title bestowed upon Gaius and
     Lucius.
   parma, -ae, f., *small, round shield.*
8 **argenteus, -a, -um,** *made of silver.*
   dōnātum: translate, *presented with.*

1 §13 Iānum Quirīnum, quem claussum esse maiōrēs nostrī
2 voluērunt, cum per tōtum imperium populī Rōmānī terrā
3 marīque esset parta victōriīs pāx, cum prius, quam nāscerer, ā
4 conditā urbe bis omnīnō clausum fuisse prōdātur memoriae, ter
5 mē prīncipe senātus claudendum esse cēnsuit.

1 §14 Fīliōs meōs, quōs iuvenēs mihi ēripuit fortūna, Gāium et
2 Lūcium Caesarēs honōris meī caussā senātus populusque
3 Rōmānus annum quīntum et decimum agentīs cōnsulēs
4 dēsignāvit, ut eum magistrātum inīrent post quīnquennium. Et
5 ex eō diē quō dēductī sunt in Forum, ut interessent cōnsiliīs
6 pūblicīs dēcrēvit senātus. Equitēs autem Rōmānī ūniversī
7 prīncipem iuventūtis utrumque eōrum parmīs et hastīs
8 argenteīs dōnātum appellāvērunt.

15

1   **virītim**, adv., *per man, individually.*
    HS: abbreviation for **sēstertiōs** (see the following entry).
    sēstertius, -ī, m., *sesterce* (denomination of Roman coinage).
    trecēnī, -ae, -a, *three hundred each/apiece.*
    ex testāmentō patris meī: this donation was one of the conditions of the
      will of Julius Caesar. It was given by Octavian in 44 B.C.
2   **quadringēnī, -ae, -a**, *four hundred each/apiece.*
3   **manibiae, -ārum**, f. pl., *booty, spoils.* The spelling **manubiae** is more
      common. In classical Latin there is variation between short **i** and
      short **u** in open medial syllables before labial consonants. See
      INTRODUCTION §2.1.
    cōnsul quīntum: 29 B.C. The donation was made on the occasion of his
      triple triumph. See paragraph 4, line 1.
    in cōnsulātū decimō: 24 B.C. The third donation was given after
      Augustus returned from the war in Spain.
4   **patrimōnium, -ī**, n., *inheritence.*
    congiārium, -ī, n., *money distributed as a gift, largess, gratuity.*
    congiārī: gen. sg.
5   **pernumerō, -āre, -āvī, -ātum**, *to count out, pay over.*
    ūndecimum, adv., *for the eleventh time.*
    cōnsul ūndecimum: 23 B.C. See paragraph 5, lines 3–6 for the circum-
      stances.
6   **frūmentātiō, frūmentātiōnis**, f., *distribution of grain; a ration of grain.*
    coemō, coemere, coēmī, coēmptum, *to buy up, purchase.*
    ēmētior, ēmētīrī, ēmēnsus, *to measure out, distribute by measure.*
7   **duodecimum**, adv., *for the twelfth time.*
    tribūniciā potestāte duodecimum: = *in the twelfth year of my tribunician
      power*, i.e., 11 B.C.
    nummus, -ī, m., *sesterce* (denomination of Roman coinage).
9   **minus**: note that **quam** is missing from this comparative construction.
10 **duodēvīcēnsimum**, adv., *for the eighteenth time.*
    Tribūniciae potestātis duodēvīcēnsimum: 5 B.C., the year Augustus'
      adopted grandson Gaius was introduced in the Forum. See para-
      graph 14.
11 **vīgintī**, *twenty.*
    plēbs, plēbis, m., *plebeians, people.* Compare the genitive **plēbī** in para-
      graph 12, line 2.
    sexāgēnī, -ae, -a, *sixty each/apiece.*
12 **colōnus, -ī**, m., *colonist.*
13 **nummum**: gen. pl.
    singulī, -ae, -a, *one apiece.*
    triumphālis, -is, -e, *triumphal.*

1 §15 Plēbēī Rōmānae virītim HS trecēnōs numerāvī ex

2 testāmentō patris meī, et nōmine meō HS quadringēnōs ex

3 bellōrum manibiīs cōnsul quīntum dedī, iterum autem in

4 cōnsulātū decimō ex patrimōniō meō HS quadringēnōs congiārī

5 virītim pernumerāvī, et cōnsul ūndecimum duodecim

6 frūmentātiōnēs frūmentō prīvātim coēmptō ēmēnsus sum, et

7 tribūniciā potestāte duodecimum quadringēnōs nummōs

8 tertium virītim dedī. Quae mea congiāria pervēnērunt ad

9 hominum mīllia numquam minus quīnquāgintā et ducenta.

10 Tribūniciae potestātis duodēvīcēnsimum, cōnsul XII, trecentīs

11 et vīgintī mīllibus plēbis urbānae sexāgēnōs dēnāriōs virītim

12 dedī. Et colōnīs mīlitum meōrum cōnsul quīntum ex manibiīs

13 virītim mīllia nummum singula dedī; accēpērunt id triumphāle

14 congiārium in colōnīs hominum circiter centum et vīgintī mīllia.

15 Cōnsul tertium decimum sexāgēnōs dēnāriōs plēbēī quae tum

16 frūmentum pūblicum accipiēbat dedī; ea mīllia hominum

17 paullō plūra quam ducenta fuērunt.

---

14 **in colōnīs**: = **in colōniīs** (cf. **colōnīs**, dat. pl. of **colōnus** *colonist*, in line 12).

15 **Cōnsul tertium decimum**: 2 B.C. In this year Augustus' second adopted grandson, Lucius, was introduced in the Forum. See paragraph 14.

16

1 **in cōnsulātū meō quārtō**: 30 B.C.

2 **M. Crassō et Cn. Lentulō Augure**: Marcus Crassus and Gnaeus Lentulus
   Augur, consuls in 14 B.C.

3 **mūnicipīs**: = **mūnicipiīs**.
   summa, -ae, f., *total number/amount*.
   sēstertium: gen. pl.

4 **sexsiēns** = **sexiēns**, adv., *sixty times*.
   mīlliēns, adv., *one thousand times*.
   sēstertium circiter sexsiēns mīlliēns: in order to indicate sums of money
   over a million, numeral adverbs are combined with a noun phrase
   centēna mīllia, which is often omitted. Thus, the sum of money is
   6,000 x 100,000 (**centēna mīllia**) **sēstertium** (genitive plural) =
   600,000,000 *of sesterces*. The noun phrase **centēna mīllia** must also be
   understood with the numeral adverbs in lines 4 and 13 below and in
   paragraph 17, lines 1–2, 5–6.
   praedium, -ī, n., *portion of land*.
   praedīs: = **praediīs**.

5 **sescentiēns**, adv., *six hundred times*.
   quod: the antecedent here is **bis mīlliēns et sescentiēns (centēna mīllia)**;
   compare **quam** (line 4), the antecedent of which is **ea summa** (line 3).
   prōvinciālis, -is, -e, *of a province*.

7 **prōvincīs**: = **prōvinciīs**.
   aetās, aetātis, f., *age, lifetime*.

8 **Ti. Nerōne et Cn. Pīsōne**: Tiberius Nero and Gnaeus Piso, consuls in 7
   B.C.
   C. Antistiō et D. Laeliō: Gaius Antistius and Decimus Laelius, consuls in
   6 B.C.

9 **C. Calvisiō et L. Pasiēnō**: Gaius Calvisius and Lucius Pasienuṣ, consuls
   in 4 B.C.

10 **L. Lentulō et M. Messallā**: Lucius Lentulus and Marcus Messalla,
   consuls in 3 B.C.
   L. Canīniō et Q. Fabriciō: Lucius Caninius and Quintus Fabricius,
   consuls in 2 B.C.

11 **ēmeriteis**: **ei** is a spelling for **ī**. There are several examples of this
   spelling in the **Rēs Gestae**, e.g., **quadrīgeis** paragraph 24, line 4,
   Dalmateis paragraph 29, line 2. See INTRODUCTION §2.1.
   stīpendīs: = **stīpendiīs**.

12 **numerātum, -ī**, n., *cash, money*.
   persolvō, persolvere, persolvī, persolūtum, *to give/pay out*.

13 **quater**, adv., *four times*.
   impendō, impendere, impendī, impēnsum, *to pay out, spend*.

1 §16 Pecūniam prō agrīs quōs in cōnsulātū meō quārtō et posteā

2 cōnsulibus M. Crassō et Cn. Lentulō Augure adsignāvī

3 mīlitibus solvī mūnicipīs. Ea summa sēstertium circiter

4 sexsiēns mīlliēns fuit, quam prō Italicīs praedīs numerāvī, et

5 circiter bis mīlliēns et sescentiēns, quod prō agrīs prōvinciālibus

6 solvī. Id prīmus et sōlus omnium quī dēdūxērunt colōniās

7 mīlitum in Italiā aut in prōvincīs ad memoriam aetātis meae

8 fēcī. Et posteā Ti. Nerōne et Cn. Pīsōne cōnsulibus, itemque C.

9 Antistiō et D. Laeliō cōs. et C. Calvisiō et L. Pasiēnō cōnsulibus

10 et L. Lentulō et M. Messallā cōnsulibus et L. Canīniō et Q.

11 Fabriciō cōs., mīlitibus quōs ēmeriteis stīpendīs in sua

12 mūnicipia dēdūxī praemia numerātō persolvī, quam in rem

13 sēstertium quater mīlliēns circiter impendī.

17

1   **iuvō, iuvāre, iūvī, iūtum,** *to assist.*
    aerārium, -ī, n., *public treasury.*
2   **quīngentiēns,** adv., *five hundred times.*
    ad eōs: between 28 and 23 B.C. the Treasury was supervised by two
      prefects; from 23 B.C. two praetors were in charge.
    praesum, praeesse, praefuī + dat., *to be in charge of.*
    praerant: = **praeerant.**
3   **M. Lepidō et L. Arruntiō:** Marcus Lepidus and Lucius Arruntius,
      consuls in A.D. 6.
    mīlitāris, -is, -e, *belonging to the military.*
    aerārium mīlitāre: the military Treasury was founded by Augustus in
      A.D. 6. The money was used to reward soldiers discharged from
      military service.
    ex cōnsiliō meō: *on my advice.*
4   **ex quō ... darentur:** a relative clause of purpose, *so that from it . . . might
      be given.*
5   **vīcēnī, -ae, -a,** *twenty apiece.*
    stīpendia ēmeruissent: *had served out twenty or more years of military
      service.* See paragraph 3, lines 9–10.
    ēmeruissent: subjunctive by "attraction" to **darentur** in line 4.
6   **septingentiēns,** adv., *seven hundred times.*

18

1   **Cn. et P. Lentulī:** Gnaeus Lentulus and Publius Lentulus, consuls in 18
      B.C.
2   **dēficiō, dēficere, dēfēcī, dēfectum,** *to be lacking, be insufficient.*
    vectīgāl, vectīgālis, n., *revenue derived from public property, income.*
    tum ... tum, adv., *at one time . . . at another time; sometimes . . . sometimes.*
3   **frūmentārius, -a, -um,** *consisting of grain.*
    nummārius, -a, -um, *consisting of money.*
    tribūtus, -ūs, m., *allocation, apportionment, distribution.*
    horreum, -ī, n., *granary.*
4   **ēdō, ēdere, ēdidī, ēditum,** *to give out.*

1 **§17** Quater pecūniā meā iūvī aerārium, ita ut sēstertium
2 mīlliēns et quīngentiēns ad eōs quī praerant aerāriō dētulerim.
3 Et M. Lepidō et L. Arruntiō cōs. in aerārium mīlitāre quod ex
4 cōnsiliō meō cōnstitūtum est, ex quō praemia darentur
5 mīlitibus quī vīcēna aut plūra stīpendia ēmeruissent, HS
6 mīlliēns et septingentiēns ex patrimōniō meō dētulī.

1 **§18** Ab eō annō quō Cn. et P. Lentulī cōnsulēs fuērunt, cum
2 dēficerent vectīgālia, tum centum mīllibus hominum tum
3 plūribus multō frūmentāriōs et nummāriōs tribūtūs ex horreō
4 et patrimōniō meō ēdidī.

acc pl?

"by & many"

ablative of degree
of difference

19

1   **Cūria, -ae**, f., *Senate-House* (the so-called Curia Julia).
    continēns, continentis + dat., *adjacent to, next to, close to*.
    Chalcidicum, -ī, n., *Chalcidicum* (a courtyard adjoining the Senate-
        House).
    Apollō, Apollinis, m., *Apollo* (god of prophecy, music, poetry).
2   **Palātium, -ī**, n., *Palatine Hill*.
    porticus, -ūs, f., *colonnade, portico*.
    Iūlius, -ī, m., *Julius* (family name of Gaius Julius Caesar).
    Cūriam . . . aedem dīvī Iūliī: the Senate-House, the Chalcidicum, the
        Temple of Apollo, and the Temple of the Divine Julius [Caesar] were
        completed within the years 29 and 28 B.C.
    Lupercal, Lupercālis, n., *Lupercal*. The cave at the foot of the Palatine
        Hill where Romulus and Remus were suckled by a she-wolf.
        Augustus turned it into an ornamental grotto.
    porticum: originally built in 167 B.C. in honor of Octavius' victory over
        the fleet of Perseus of Macedon (168 B.C.), the portico was recon-
        structed by Augustus in 33 B.C. Augustus allowed it to be called the
        Octavian Portico.
3   **Circum Flāminium**: *Circus Flaminius* (a stadium for chariot-racing).
    quam sum appellārī passus . . . Octāviam: take **Octāviam** as predicate
        accusative with **appellārī**.
4   **priōrem**: supply **porticum**.
    solum, -ī, n., *foundation, base*.
    pulvīnar: a roofed box with seats from which the emperor watched the
        races at the circus. Compare this meaning with that found in
        paragraph 9, line 5.
5   **Iuppiter Feretrius, Iovis Feretrī**, m., *Jupiter Feretrius*.
    Iuppiter Tonāns, Iovis Tonantis, m., *Jupiter Tonans* (the "thunderer").
    aedēs . . . Iovis Feretrī et Iovis Tonantis: both temples were located on
        the Capitoline Hill. The Temple of Jupiter Feretrius was restored in
        31 B.C. Augustus dedicated the Temple of Jupiter Tonans in 22 B.C. to
        commemorate his narrow escape from a lightning strike while
        campaigning in Spain (26/25 B.C.)
6   **Quirīnus, -ī**, m., *Quirinus* (god worshiped on the Capitoline Hill, com-
        monly identified with the deified Romulus).
    Minerva, -ae, f., *Minerva*.
    Iūnō Rēgīna, Iūnōnis Rēgīnae, f., *Juno Regina* (the "Queen").
7   **Iuppiter Lībertās, Iovis Lībertātis**, m., *Jupiter Libertas*.
    Aventīnus, -ī, m., *Aventine Hill*.
    Sacra Via, Sacra Viae, f., *Sacra Via* (a road leading through the Forum).

dative

1 **§19** Cūriam et continēns eī Chalcidicum, templumque Apollinis

2 in Palātiō cum porticibus, aedem dīvī Iūlī, Lupercal, porticum

3 ad Circum Flāminium, quam sum appellārī passus ex nōmine

4 eius quī priōrem eōdem in solō fēcerat Octāviam, pulvīnar ad

5 Circum Maximum, aedēs in Capitōliō Iovis Feretrī et Iovis

6 Tonantis, aedem Quirīnī, aedēs Minervae et Iūnōnis Rēgīnae et

7 Iovis Lībertātis in Aventīnō, aedem Larum in summā Sacrā Viā,

8 aedem deum Penātium in Veliā, aedem Iuventātis, aedem

9 Mātris Magnae in Palātiō fēcī.

---

8 **dī Penātēs, deōrum Penātium**, m. pl., *Penates* (gods controlling the
destiny of the Roman household).
deum: gen. pl.
Velia, -ae, f., *Velia* (ridge connecting the Palatine Hill and the Oppian
Hill).
Iuventās, Iuventātis, f., *Iuventas* (goddess of youth).

9 **Māter Magna, Mātris Magnae**, f., *Magna Mater, Cybele*.

*actually
deorum
contracted*

20

1 **Capitōlium**: the temple of Jupiter Optimus Maximus. It burned down in
9 B.C. The date of its restoration is unknown.
  Pompēius, -a, -um, *of Pompey.*
  theātrum, -ī, n., *theater.*
  Pompēium theātrum: the Theater of Pompey was the first stone theater
in Rome. Construction was completed in 55 B.C.
  utrumque opus: this phrase is in apposition with **Capitōlium et
Pompēium theātrum.**
2 **grandis, -is, -e**, *great.*
  īnscrīptiō, īnscrīptiōnis, f., *inscription.*
  rīvus, -ī, m., *conduit, channel, watercourse.*
3 **aqua, -ae**, f., *water; aqueduct.*
  vetustās, vetustātis, f., *old age.*
  Mārcius, -a, -um, *Marcian.*
  aquam quae Mārcia appellātur: reconstruction took place in 5-4 B.C.
4 **duplicō, -āre, -āvī, -ātum**, *to double* (the capacity of).
5 **Forum Iūlium**: the Forum of Julius Caesar.
  basilica, -ae, f., *basilica* (hall used as a law-court).
  basilicam: the Basilica Julia.
6 **Castor, Castoris**, m., *Castor* (god of merchants).
  Sāturnus, -ī, m., *Saturn* (god of agriculture).
  coepī, coepisse, coeptum, *to begin.*
  prōflīgō, -āre, -āvī, -ātum, *to be in a nearly completed state.*
  coepta prōflīgātaque opera: this phrase is in apposition with **Forum
Iūlium et basilicam.**
  ā patre meō: Julius Caesar.
7 **cōnsūmō, cōnsūmere, cōnsūmpsī, cōnsūmptum**, *to destroy; to wear away;
to consume.*
8 **ampliō, -āre, -āvī, -ātus**, *to extend, increase.*
  titulus, -ī, m., *commemorative inscription.*
9 **incohō, -āre, -āvī, -ātum**, *to start work on.*
  sī . . . nōn perfēcissem: pluperfect subjunctive for future perfect indicative in secondary sequence, *if I would not have. . . .*
10 **octōgintā**, *eighty.*
  sextum, adv., *for the sixth time.*
11 **praetermittō, praetermittere, praetermīsī, praetermissum**, *to leave out,
omit, neglect.*
12 **Via Flāminia, Viae Flāminiae**, f., *Via Flaminia* (road leading from Rome
to Ariminum). The road was rebuilt in 27 B.C.

1 §20 Capitōlium et Pompēium theātrum utrumque opus *acc sing in* *appō to theātrum*

2 impēnsā grandī refēcī sine ūllā īnscrīptiōne nōminis meī. Rīvōs

3 aquārum complūribus locīs vetustāte lābentēs refēcī, et aquam

4 quae Mārcia appellātur duplicāvī fonte novō in rīvum eius

5 inmissō. Forum Iūlium et basilicam quae fuit inter aedem

6 Castoris et aedem Sāturnī, coepta prōflīgātaque opera ā patre

7 meō, perfēcī et eandem basilicam cōnsūmptam incendiō

8 ampliātō eius solō, sub titulō nōminis fīliōrum meōrum

9 incohāvī, et, sī vīvus nōn perfēcissem, perficī ab hērēdibus meīs

10 iussī. Duo et octōgintā templa deum in urbe cōnsul sextum ex

11 auctōritāte senātūs refēcī, nūllō praetermissō quod eō tempore

12 reficī dēbēbat. Cōnsul septimum Viam Flāminiam ab urbe

13 Arīminum refēcī pontēsque omnēs praeter Mulvium et

14 Minucium.

---

13 **Arīminum, -ī**, n., *Ariminum* (town in Umbria).
 Mulvium: understand **pontem** (bridge carrying the Via Flaminia across
  the Tiber River).

14 **Minucium**: understand **pontem** (the location of this bridge is unknown).

21

1   **solum, -ī**, n., *ground; property.* Compare paragraph 19, line 4.

    Mārtis Ultōris: *of Mars Ultor* (the "Avenger"). Augustus vowed this temple after the Republicans were defeated at Philippi in 42 B.C. It was built in the Forum of Augustus and dedicated in 2 B.C.

    forum . . . Augustum: the Forum of Augustus.

2   **Theātrum**: the Theater of Marcellus was completed in 11 B.C.

3   **quod . . . esset**: relative clause of characteristic.

    M. Mārcellī: Marcus Marcellus was the son of Augustus' sister, Octavia, and the first husband of Augustus' daughter, Julia. He died in 23 B.C.

4   **gener, generī**, m., *son-in-law.*

    Capitōliō: see paragraph 20, line 1.

5   **Vesta, -ae**, f., *Vesta* (goddess of the domestic hearth).

6   **cōnstō, cōnstāre, cōnstitī** + dat. of person making the expenditure, *to cost.*

7   **corōnārius, -a, -um**, *used for making crowns or wreaths.*

    Aurī corōnārī: gen. sg. Gold crowns were awarded to triumphant generals.

    pondō, adv., *in weight, by weight.*

    pondō trīgintā et quīnque mīllia: understand **lībrārum** [**lībra, -ae**, f., *a balance, pair of scales; a pound* (measure of weight)], *of pounds* as partitive genitive with **mīllia**.

9   **quotiēnscumque**, conj., *as often as.*

10 **dēcernentibus mūnicipiīs et colōnīs**: the ablative absolute is concessive in function.

11 **colōnīs**: = **colōniīs**.

    aequē, adv., *equally.*

    benignē, adv., *kindly.*

    adque = **atque**, conj., *as.*

    aequē benignē adque: translate *as kindly as.*

1 **§21** In prīvātō solō Mārtis Ultōris templum forumque

2 Augustum ex manibiīs fēcī. Theātrum ad aedem Apollinis in

3 solō magnā ex parte ā prīvātīs ēmptō fēcī, quod sub nōmine M.

4 Mārcellī generī meī esset. Dōna ex manibiīs in Capitōliō et in

5 aede dīvī Iūlī et in aede Apollinis et in aede Vestae et in templō

6 Mārtis Ultōris cōnsacrāvī, quae mihi cōnstitērunt HS circiter

7 mīlliēns. Aurī corōnārī pondō trīgintā et quīnque mīllia

8 mūnicipiīs et colōnīs Italiae cōnferentibus ad triumphōs meōs

9 quīntum cōnsul remīsī, et posteā, quotiēnscumque imperātor

10 appellātus sum, aurum corōnārium nōn accēpī dēcernentibus

11 mūnicipiīs et colōnīs aequē benignē adque anteā dēcrēverant.

22

1 **gladiātōrius, -a, -um,** *gladiatorial.*

    mūnus gladiātōrium: Augustus is known to have sponsored gladiatorial shows in the following years: 29, 28, 16, 12, 7, 2 B.C. , and A.D. 6. The date of the eighth show is uncertain.

    fīliōrum . . . nōmine: Augustus' adopted sons were Gaius and Lucius Caesar (17 B.C.), Agrippa Postumus (A.D. 4), and Tiberius (A.D. 4); his grandsons were Germanicus, son of the elder Drusus, and Drusus, son of Tiberius.

3 **dēpugnō, -āre, -āvī, -ātum,** *to do battle, fight in the arena.*

    athlēta, -ae, m., *athlete.*

4 **acciō, acciere, acciī/accīvī, accītum,** *to send for, invite, summon.*

5 **nepōtis meī nōmine:** Augustus is referring to either Germanicus or Drusus.

6 **vicem,** adv. + preceding gen., *in place of, on behalf of.*

    conlēgium: = **collēgium.** For the spelling compare **conlēgam** paragraph 6, line 7.

7 **XVvirōrum:** compare paragraph 7, line 4.

    lūdī saec(u)lārēs, lūdōrum saec(u)lārium, m. pl., *secular games.* This festival, instituted to mark the end of one century (**saeclum**) and the beginning of another, was celebrated by Augustus in 17 B.C. as a means of inaugurating Rome's new golden era. The festival was celebrated in a poem by Horace (*Carmen Saeculare*).

8 **C. Furniō C. Sīlānō cōs.:** Gaius Furnius and Gaius Silanus, consuls in 17 B.C.

    Cōnsul XIII: 2 B.C.

    lūdōs Mārtiālēs: these games were held by Augustus in 2 B.C. in order to celebrate the dedication of the Temple of Mars Ultor.

9 **deinceps,** adv., *in succession.*

    īnsequor, īnsequī, īnsecūtus, *to follow after.*

10 **s.c.:** = **senātūs cōnsultō.**

    vēnātiō, vēnātiōnis, f., *animal-hunt.*

    Vēnātiōnēs: the hunts were sponsored in 11 B.C., 2 B.C., and A.D. 12.

11 **Āfricānus, -a, -um,** *African.*

12 **amphitheātrum, -ī,** n., *amphitheater.*

13 **cōnficiō, cōnficere, cōnfēcī, cōnfectum,** *to kill, destroy.*

    bēstiārum circiter tria mīllia et quīngentae: quīngentae is feminine, nominative, plural, in agreement with the gender and number of **bēstiārum.**

1 §22 Ter mūnus gladiātōrium dedī meō nōmine et quīnquiēns

2 fīliōrum meōrum aut nepōtum nōmine, quibus mūneribus

3 dēpugnāvērunt hominum circiter decem mīllia. Bis athlētārum

4 undique accītōrum spectāculum populō praebuī meō nōmine et

5 tertium nepōtis meī nōmine. Lūdōs fēcī meō nōmine quater,

6 aliōrum autem magistrātuum vicem ter et vīciēns. Prō conlēgiō

7 XVvirōrum magister conlēgiī collēgā M. Agrippā lūdōs saeclārēs

8 C. Furniō C. Sīlānō cōs. fēcī. Cōnsul XIII lūdōs Mārtiālēs

9 prīmus fēcī, quōs post id tempus deinceps īnsequentibus annīs

10 s.c. et lēge fēcērunt cōnsulēs. Vēnātiōnēs bēstiārum

11 Āfricānārum meō nōmine aut fīliōrum meōrum et nepōtum in

12 circō aut in forō aut in amphitheātrīs populō dedī sexiēns et

13 vīciēns, quibus cōnfecta sunt bēstiārum circiter tria mīllia et

14 quīngentae.

23

1 **nāvālis, -is, -e**, *involving ships.*
   spectāc(u)lum: = **spectaculum**. The show was sponsored in 2 B.C. as part
    of the celebration inaugurating the Temple of Mars Ultor.
   in quō locō: the antecedent **locō** is incorporated into its relative clause.
2 **nemus, nemoris**, n., *woods, forest, grove.*
   nemus . . . Caesarum: located across the Tiber River, opposite the
    Aventine Hill.
   cavō, -āre, -āvī, -ātum, *to dig out.*
3 **longitūdō, longitūdinis**, f., *length.*
   mīlle et octingentōs pedēs: accusative of extent of space.
   lātitūdō, lātitūdinis, f., *width.*
4 **ducentī**: the nominative is an error for **ducentōs (pedēs)**. Compare this
    to the phrase **mīlle et octingentōs pedēs** in line 3.
   rōstrātus, -a, -um, *provided with a beak.*
   birēmis, -is, -e, *having two oars to each bench or room.*
5 **cōnflīgō, cōnflīgere, cōnflīxī, cōnflīctum**, *to clash, do battle.*
   classis, classis, f., *fleet.*
6 **rēmex, rēmigis**, m., *rower.*

24

1 **cīvitātium**: this noun is a consonant-stem. Note the i-stem genitive
    plural ending **-ium** here.
   Asia, -ae, f., *Asia.*
   victor: i.e., at Actium.
2 **ōrnāmentum, -ī**, n., *ornament; religious relic.*
   repōnō, repōnere, reposuī, repositum, *to put back.*
   spoliō, -āre, -āvī, -ātum, *to plunder, pillage.*
   is cum quō bellum gesseram: Mark Antony.
3 **possideō, possidēre, possēdī, possessum**, *to appropriate.*
   pedester, pedestris, pedestre, *pedestrian, going on foot.*
4 **equester, equestris, equestre**, *equestrian, going on horseback.*
   quadrīga, -ae, f., *chariot with its team of four horses.*
   quadrīgeis: = **quadrīgīs**.
5 **tollō, tollere, sustulī, sublātum**, *to remove.*
   exque eā pecūnia: i.e., the money obtained from the sale of these statues.
   aureus, -a, -um, *made of gold.*
6 **mihi statuārum honōrem habuērunt**: *paid me the honor of having set up
    statues to me.*

1 §23 Nāvālis proelī spectāclum populō dedī trāns Tiberim, in

2 quō locō nunc nemus est Caesarum, cavātō solō in

3 longitūdinem mīlle et octingentōs pedēs, in lātitūdinem mīlle et

4 ducentī. In quō trīgintā rōstrātae nāvēs trirēmēs aut birēmēs,

5 plūrēs autem minōrēs inter sē cōnflīxērunt. Quibus in classibus

6 pugnāvērunt praeter rēmigēs mīllia hominum tria circiter.

1 §24 In templīs omnium cīvitātium prōvinciae Asiae victor

2 ōrnāmenta reposuī, quae spoliātīs templīs is cum quō bellum

3 gesseram prīvātim possēderat. Statuae meae pedestrēs et

4 equestrēs et in quadrīgeis argenteae stetērunt in urbe XXC

5 circiter, quās ipse sustulī exque eā pecūniā dōna aurea in aede

6 Apollinis meō nōmine et illōrum quī mihi statuārum honōrem

7 habuērunt posuī.

25

1 **pācō, -āre, -āvī, -ātum**, *to bring under control.*

    praedō, praedōnis, m., *pirate.*

    Mare . . . praedōnibus: this refers to Augustus' naval victory over Sextus Pompeius in 36 B.C.

    servōrum: partitive genitive with **trīgintā . . . mīllia**; Pompeius' ships were manned by slaves.

3 **fere**, adv., *almost.*

    capta: agreeing with **mīllia**.

    supplicium, -ī, n., *punishment.*

    ad supplicium sūmendum: gerundive with **ad** to express purpose, *for the purpose of exacting punishment.*

4 **Iūrāvit in mea verba**: *took an oath of allegiance to me.*

    sponte suā: *of its own accord.*

5 **Actium, -ī**, n., *Actium* (a promontory north of Acarnania, a state in northwest Greece). Octavian and Antony waged a sea battle off the coast of Actium in September, 31 B.C.

6 **Galliae, -ārum**, f. pl., *the provinces of Gaul.*

    Hispāniae, -ārum, f. pl., *the provinces of Spain.*

    Āfrica, -ae, f., *Roman province of Africa.*

    Sicilia, -ae, f., *Sicily.*

    Sardinia, -ae, f., *Sardinia.*

    prōvinciae . . . Sardinia: these were the provinces under the control of Octavian per his agreement with Antony (who received the eastern provinces) at Brundisium in 40 B.C.

    Quī: the antecedent is **senātōrēs plūrēs quam DCC**.

7 **signum, -ī**, n., *military standard.*

    mīlitō, -āre, -āvī, -ātum, *to perform military service, serve* (as a soldier).

    mīlitāverint: subjunctive in a relative clause of characteristic.

    senātōrēs: those who supported Octavian in his campaign against Antony.

8 **in iīs quī**: understand **erant**, i.e., **in iīs [erant] LXXXIII quī**.

1 §25 Mare pācāvī ā praedōnibus. Eō bellō servōrum quī fūgerant

2 ā dominīs suīs et arma contrā rem pūblicam cēperant, trīgintā

3 ferē mīllia capta dominīs ad supplicium sūmendum trādidī.

4 Iūrāvit in mea verba tōta Italia sponte suā, et mē bellī quō vīcī

5 ad Actium ducem dēpoposcit. Iūrāvērunt in eadem verba

6 prōvinciae Galliae, Hispāniae, Āfrica, Sicilia, Sardinia. Quī sub

7 signīs meīs tum mīlitāverint, fuērunt senātōrēs plūrēs quam

8 DCC, in iīs quī vel anteā vel posteā cōnsulēs factī sunt ad eum

9 diem quō scrīpta sunt haec, LXXXIII, sacerdōtēs circiter CLXX.

26

1 **fīnitimus, -a, -um**, *situated/living on the boundary; adjacent to* + dat.
2 **parērent**: subjunctive in a relative clause of characteristic.
3 **item**, adv., *also.*
  quā, rel. adv., *wherever.*
  inclūdō, inclūdere, inclūsī, inclūsum, *to bound, surround, enclose.*
  Germānia, -ae, f., *Germany.*
  Galliās . . . Germāniam: Augustus sponsored military campaigns in
    Gaul between 27 and 25 B.C., in Spain between 27 and 19 B.C., and in
    Germany between 12 and 6 B.C.
4 **Ōceanus, -ī**, m., *ocean.*
  ōstium, -ī, n., *mouth* (of a river).
  Albis, Albis, f., *Elbe* (river in Germany).
  flūmen, flūminis, n., *river.*
  Alpēs, Alpium, f. pl., *Alps.*
  Alpēs: Alpine tribes were conquered between 35 and 7 B.C.
5 **regiō, regiōnis**, f., *region.*
  Hadriānus, -a, -um, *Adriatic.*
  Tuscus, -a, -um, *Etruscan.*
  Tuscum: supply **mare** = the Tyrrhenian Sea.
6 **fēcī**: translate, *I caused* + accusative + infinitive.
  iniūria, -ae, f., *unjust treatment.*
  per iniūriam: *unjustly.*
  Classis mea: the fleet sailed the North Sea in 5 B.C. under the leadership
    of Tiberius.
7 **Rhēnus, -ī**, m., *Rhine* (river in Germany).
8 **Cimbrī, -ōrum**, m. pl., *Cimbri* (Germanic tribe).
  quō, rel. adv., *to which place.*
9 **adīt**: = **adiit**.
10 **Charydēs, Charydum**, m. pl., *Charydes* (Germanic tribe).
  Semnōnēs, Semnōnum, m. pl., *Semnones* (Germanic tribe).
  tractus, -ūs, m., *region.*
  Germānī, -ōrum, m. pl., *Germans.*
11 **amīcitia, -ae**, f., *friendship.*
13 **Aethiopia, -ae**, f., *Aethiopia.*
  in Aethiopiam: from 24 to 22 B.C. an expedition was led by Gaius
    Petronius against the queen of the Ethiopians.
  Arabia, -ae, f., *Arabia.*
  in Arabiam: the campaign in Arabia was conducted by the Egyptian
    prefect Gaius Aelius Gallus in 25–24 B.C.
14 **Eudaemōn, Eudaemōnis**, f., *Eudaemon* = *Arabia Felix* (the southern part
    of Arabia).
  cōpia, -ae, f., *supply;* pl. *troops, forces.*

1 §26 Omnium prōvinciārum populī Rōmānī, quibus fīnitimae
2 fuērunt gentēs quae nōn parērent imperiō nostrō, fīnēs auxī.
3 Galliās et Hispāniās prōvinciās, item Germāniam, quā inclūdit
4 Ōceanus ā Gādibus ad ōstium Albis flūminis, pacāvī. Alpēs ā
5 regiōne eā, quae proxima est Hadriānō marī, ad Tuscum pācārī
6 fēcī nūllī gentī bellō per iniūriam inlātō. Classis mea per
7 Ōceanum ab ōstiō Rhēnī ad sōlis orientis regiōnem usque ad
8 fīnēs Cimbrōrum nāvigāvit, quō neque terrā neque marī
9 quisquam Rōmānus ante id tempus adīt, Cimbrīque et
10 Charydēs et Semnōnēs et eiusdem tractūs aliī Germānōrum
11 populī per lēgātōs amīcitiam meam et populī Rōmānī petiērunt.
12 Meō iussū et auspiciō ductī sunt duo exercitūs eōdem ferē
13 tempore in Aethiopiam et in Arabiam, quae appellātur
14 Eudaemōn, maximaeque hostium gentis utrīusque cōpiae
15 caesae sunt in aciē et complūra oppida capta. In Aethiopiam
16 usque ad oppidum Nabata perventum est, cui proxima est
17 Meroē; in Arabiam usque in fīnēs Sabaeōrum prōcessit exercitus
18 ad oppidum Mariba.

---

15 **caedō, caedere, cecīdī, caesum,** *to cut down, slaughter.*
16 **Nabata**, gender and declension unknown, *Nabata* (the northern capital of Ethiopia). Accusative singular in apposition with **oppidum**.
   perventum est: impersonal passive of an intransitive verb, *an advance was made*; i.e. *the Roman army advanced.*
17 **Meroē, Meroēs,** f., *Meroe* (the southern capitol of Ethiopia).
   Sabaeī, -ōrum, m. pl., *Sabaeans* (a people of southwestern Arabia).
18 **Mariba**, gender and declension unknown, *Mariba* (a city of the Sabaeans in southwestern Arabia). Accusative singular in apposition with **oppidum**.

27

1   **Aegyptus, -ī**, f., *Egypt*.
    Aegyptum: Augustus took control of Egypt in 30 B.C. after the death of
    Antony and Cleopatra.
    adiciō, adicere, adiēcī, adiectum + acc. + dat., *to add to*.
    Armenia, -ae, f., *Armenia*.
    Armeniam maiōrem: this is the territory between the Black Sea and the
    Caspian sea. Lesser Armenia is located south of the Black Sea
    between Pontus and Cappadocia, and to the west of Greater Arme-
    nia.

2   **interficiō, interficere, interfēcī, interfectum**, *to kill*.
    Artaxēs, Artaxis, m., *Artaxes* (son of Artavasdes). He came to power
    after the death of Antony. He was assassinated in 20 B.C.

4   **Tigrānēs, Tigrānis**, m., *Tigranes II* (son of Artavasdes, younger brother of
    Artaxes, and grandson of Tigranes I). Augustus directed Tiberius to
    install him as ruler, which was accomplished after the murder of
    Artaxes.
    Artavasdēs, Artavasdis, m., *Artavasdes* (son of Tigranes II). He suc-
    ceeded his father, Tigranes I, in 56 B.C. Artavasdes betrayed Antony
    during Antony's campaign against the Parthians and so was re-
    moved from the throne in 34 B.C.
    Tigrānēs, Tigrānis, m., *Tigranes I* (father of Artavasdes II).
    The genealogy of the Armenian royal family is as follows: Tigranes I
    (died 56 B.C.) => Artavasdes (removed from throne in 34 B.C.) =>
    Artaxes (assassinated 20 B.C.) => Tigranes II (installed by Augustus
    in 20 B.C.; died in 7 B.C.) => Tigranes III (installed in A.D. 6, after the
    death of the Mede Artavasdes [see below, lines 7–9]).

5   **Ti. Nerōnem**: Tiberius Nero.
    prīvignus, -ī, m., *stepson*.

6   **dēscīscō, dēscīscere, dēscīvī, dēscītum**, *to revolt*.
    rebellō, -āre, -āvī, -ātum, *to rebel*.
    domō, domāre, domuī, domitum, *to subdue*.
    Gāium: peace was restored in Armenia in A.D. 2.

7   **Ariobarzānēs, Ariobarzānis**, m., *Ariobarzanes* (son of Artabazes, king of
    Media). He became king of Armenia in A.D. 3.
    Mēdī, -ōrum, m. pl., *the Medes*.
    Artabazus, Artabazī, m., *Artabazus* (king of Media, father of
    Ariobarzanes).

8   **Artavasdēs, Artavasdis**, m., *Artavasdes* (son of the Mede
    Ariobarzanes).

9   **Tigrānēs, Tigrānis**, m., *Tigranes III*.
    Tigrānem: Tigranes III became king in A.D. 6, after the assassination of
    Artavasdes the Mede.
    Armeniī, -ōrum, m. pl., *the Armenians*.

1   §27 Aegyptum imperiō populī Rōmānī adiēcī. Armeniam

2   maiōrem interfectō rēge eius Artaxe cum possem facere

3   prōvinciam, māluī maiōrum nostrōrum exemplō rēgnum id

4   Tigrānī rēgis Artavasdis fīliō, nepōtī autem Tigrānis rēgis, per

5   Ti. Nerōnem trādere, quī tum mihi prīvignus erat. Et eandem

6   gentem posteā dēscīscentem et rebellantem domitam per Gāium

7   fīlium meum rēgī Ariobarzānī, rēgis Mēdōrum Artabazī fīliō,

8   regendam trādidī, et post eius mortem fīliō eius Artavasdī; quō

9   interfectō Tigrānem, quī erat ex rēgiō genere Armeniōrum

10   oriundus, in id rēgnum mīsī. Prōvinciās omnīs, quae trāns

11   Hadriānum mare vergunt ad Orientem, Cȳrēnāsque, iam ex

12   parte magnā rēgibus ea possidentibus, et anteā Siciliam et

13   Sardiniam occupātās bellō servīlī reciperāvī.

---

10   **oriundus, -a, -um**, *descended from.*

    prōvinciās . . . Cȳrēnāsque: the provinces from Macedonia eastward (Achaea, Cilicia, Bithynia, Syria, etc.) were ceded to Antony by the agreement at Brundisium (40 B.C.). Octavian "recovered" them after the battle of Actium.

11   **vergō, -ere**, *to look to, point towards.*

    Cȳrēnae, -ārum, f. pl., *Cyrene.*

    iam . . . rēgibus . . . possidentibus: ablative absolute.

12   **ea**: the neuter plural refers back to **prōvinciās omnīs . . . Cȳrēnāsque**.

    Siciliam et Sardiniam: Octavian took control of these provinces (in 36 B.C. and 38 B.C. respectively) after defeating Sextus Pompeius.

13   **servīlis, -is, -e**, *of slaves.*

    bellō servīlī: ablative of time when. Augustus refers to naval battles against Sextus Pompeius. See paragraph 25.

28

1 **Macedonia, -ae**, f., *Macedonia*.
2 **Achāia, -ae**, f., *Achaia*.
  Gallia Narbōnēnsis, Galliae Narbōnēnsis, f., *Gallia Narbonensis*.
  Pisidia, -ae, f., *Pisidia* (a region in the southern part of Asia Minor).
  mīlitum: this noun depends on **Colōniās**.
3 **celeber, celebris, celebre**, *populous*.
4 **frequēns, frequentis**, *densely packed, crowded*.

29

1 **āmittō, āmittere, āmīsī, āmissum**, *to lose*.
  dēvincō, dēvincere, dēvīcī, dēvictum, *to defeat decisively, subdue*.
2 **recēpī**: in 34 B.C. Octavian recovered the Roman standards that had been lost to the Dalmatians by Gabinius (48 B.C.) and Vatinius (44 B.C.). It is not clear when the standards were lost in Spain and Gaul nor when they were recovered.
  Dalmatae, -ārum, m. pl., *the Dalmatians*.
  Dalmateis: = **Dalmatīs**.
  Parthī, -ōrum, m. pl., *the Parthians*.
3 **exercitum**: gen. pl. with contraction of **uu**, = **exercituum**.
  spolium, -ī, n., *spoils* (arms, equipment taken from a defeated enemy).
  signa: in 20 B.C. Augustus negotiated the return of Roman standards lost by Crassus (53 B.C.), Saxa (40 B.C.), and Antony (36 B.C.).
4 **supplex, supplicis**, m., *suppliant*.
5 **penetrālis, penetrālis**, n., *inner shrine*.
  penetrālī: abl. sg.

30

1 **Pannoniī, -ōrum**, m. pl., *Pannonians*.
  Pannoniōrum gentēs . . . dēvictās: Pannonia was conquered between 12 and 9 B.C. and again, after a revolt, between A.D. 6 and 9.
4 **Illyricum, -ī**, n., *Illyricum*.
  Dānuvius, -ī, m., *Danube* (river in Germany).
  Dānuī: gen. sg.
  citrā, prep. + acc., *on this side of*.
5 **Dacī, -ōrum**, m. pl., *the Dacians*.
  Dacōrum trānsgressus exercitus: the Dacian army was engaged several times by the troops of Tiberius during his Pannonian expeditions.
6 **trāns Dānuvium**: Roman troops were led across the Danube against the Dacians by the general Lentulus. The date is uncertain (between 9 B.C. and A.D. 6).
7 **perferō, perferre, pertulī, perlātum**, *to submit to, endure*.

1 **§28** Colōniās in Āfricā, Siciliā, Macedoniā, utrāque Hispāniā,

2 Achāiā, Asiā, Syriā, Galliā Narbōnēnsī, Pisidiā mīlitum dēdūxī.

3 Italia autem XXVIII colōniās, quae vīvō mē celeberrimae et

4 frequentissimae fuērunt, meā auctōritāte dēductās habet.

1 **§29** Signa mīlitāria complūra per aliōs ducēs āmissa dēvictīs

2 hostibus recēpī ex Hispāniā et Galliā et ā Dalmateis. Parthōs

3 trium exercitum Rōmānōrum spolia et signa reddere mihi

4 supplicēsque amīcitiam populī Rōmānī petere coēgī. Ea autem

5 signa in penetrālī, quod est in templō Mārtis Ultōris, reposuī.

1 **§30** Pannoniōrum gentēs, quās ante mē prīncipem populī

2 Rōmānī exercitus nunquam adīt, dēvictās per Ti. Nerōnem, quī

3 tum erat prīvignus et lēgātus meus, imperiō populī Rōmānī

4 subiēcī, prōtulīque fīnēs Illyricī ad rīpam flūminis Dānuī. Citrā

5 quod Dacōrum trānsgressus exercitus meīs auspicīs victus

6 prōflīgātusque est, et posteā trāns Dānuvium ductus exercitus

7 meus Dacōrum gentēs imperia populī Rōmānī perferre coēgit.

31

1 **India, -ae,** f., *India.*
  lēgātiō, lēgātiōnis, f., *embassy.*
2 **quisquam, quisquam, quicquam,** *any.*
3 **appetō, appetere, appetīvī, appetītum,** *to seek after.*
  Bastarnae, -ārum, m. pl., *the Bastarnians* (Germanic tribe at the mouth of the Danube).
4 **Scythēs (Scytha), -ae,** m., *a Scythian* (nomadic tribe north-east of the Black Sea).
  Sarmatae, -ārum, m. pl., *the Sarmatians.*
  Sarmatārum . . . rēgēs: the genitive **Sarmatārum** is governed by **rēgēs.** Supply **flūmen Tanaim** as the object of the preposition **ultrā.**
  Tanais, Tanais, m., *Don* (river in Sarmatia).
  ultrā, prep. + acc., *on the farther side of, beyond.*
5 **Albānī, -ōrum,** m. pl., *the Albanians* (in the Caucasus).
  Hibērī, -ōrum, m. pl., *the Iberians* (in Georgia).
  et Hibērōrum et Mēdōrum: supply **rex** as the governing noun with each of these two genitives.

32

1 **supplicēs:** in apposition with **rēgēs.**
  Tīridātēs, Tīridātae, m., *Tiridates II.* Tiridates was a pretender to the Parthian throne who sought the protection of Augustus after being expelled by King Phrates IV (c. 30 B.C.).
2 **Phrātēs, Phrātis,** m., *Phrates.* Phrates, the son of the Parthian king, was kidnapped by Tiridates and brought to Augustus in 25 B.C.
  Phrātēs, Phrātis, m., *Phrates IV.* Parthian king from whom Augustus recovered the Roman standards in 20 B.C. (see paragraph 29, lines 6–8).
  Artavasdēs: see paragraph 27, line 8.
3 **Adiabēnī, -ōrum,** m. pl., *the Adiabenians* (an Assyrian people).
  Artaxarēs, Artaxaris, m., *Artaxares* (king of the Adiabenians).
  Britannī, -ōrum, m. pl., *the Britons.*
  Dumnobellaunus, -ī, m., *Dumnobellaunus.*
4 **Tincommius, -ī,** m., *Tincommius.*
  Sugambrī, -ōrum, m. pl., *the Sugambrians* (a Germanic tribe).
  Maelō, Maelōnis, m., *Maelo.*
  Marcomanī, -ōrum, m. pl., *the Marcomanians* (a Germanic tribe).
  Suēbī, -ōrum, m. pl., *the Suebians* (Germanic tribes).
  Marcomanōrum Suēbōrum: supply a conjunction between these nouns.

1 §31 Ad mē ex Indiā rēgum lēgātiōnēs saepe missae sunt nōn
2 vīsae ante id tempus apud quemquam Rōmānōrum ducem.
3 Nostram amīcitiam appetīvērunt per lēgātōs Bastarnae
4 Scythaeque et Sarmatārum quī sunt citrā flūmen Tanaim et ultrā
5 rēgēs, Albānōrumque rēx et Hibērōrum et Mēdōrum.

1 §32 Ad mē supplicēs cōnfūgērunt rēgēs Parthōrum Tīridātēs et
2 posteā Phrātēs rēgis Phrātis fīlius, Mēdōrum Artavasdēs,
3 Adiabēnōrum Artaxarēs, Britannōrum Dumnobellaunus et
4 Tincommius, Sugambrōrum Maelō, Marcomanōrum Suēbōrum
5 . . . rus. Ad mē rēx Parthōrum Phrātēs Orōdis fīlius fīliōs suōs
6 nepōtēsque omnēs mīsit in Italiam, nōn bellō superātus, sed
7 amīcitiam nostram per līberōrum suōrum pignora petēns.
8 Plūrimaeque aliae gentēs expertae sunt p. R. fidem mē prīncipe
9 quibus anteā cum populō Rōmānō nūllum extiterat lēgātiōnum
10 et amīcitiae commercium.

---

5 **. . . rus**: the inscription is irreparably damaged at this point. All that can
   be read is the final portion of the name of the king of the
   Marcomanians and the Suebians.
   Orōdēs, Orōdis, m., *Orodes*.
   Phrātēs Orōdis fīlius: King Phrates IV. In 10 B.C. he sent his four sons to
   Rome to be educated.
7 **pignus, pignoris**, n., *pledge, surety, guarantee*.
8 **p. R.**: abbreviation for **populī Rōmānī**.
9 **ex(s)tō, exstāre, exstitī**, *to exist*.
10 **commercium, -ī**, n., *exchange*.

33

1   per lēgātōs . . . petītos: the direct object of **accēpērunt** is **rēgēs**, which is
    modified by the circumstantial participle **petītōs**, *having been sought*
    = *whom they had sought*. Take **per lēgātōs** with **petītōs**. The noun
    phrase **prīncipēs eārum gentium** stands in apposition with **lēgātōs**.

2   **Vonōnēs, Vonōnis**, m., *Vonones* (son of King Phrates IV).   He was sent
    to Rome in 10 B.C. to be educated. (see paragraph 32, line 6).   Parthian
    leaders persuaded Augustus to send him back to Parthia to be
    installed as king in A.D. 6. He was expelled in A.D. 12. He then
    ventured to Armenia where he sought to become king.

3   **Ariobarzānēs, Ariobarzānis**, m., *Ariobarzanes* (son of Artavazdes, king of
    Media); see paragraph 27, line 7 for his grandfather Ariobarzanes.

4   **Artavazdis**: = **Artavasdis**.

34

1   **In cōnsulātū sextō et septimō**: 28–27 B.C.

2   **cōnsēnsus, -ūs**, m., *consent, agreement*.
    potītus: governs the genitive noun phrase **rērum omnium**.

4   **arbitrium, -ī**, n., *dominion, control*.
    meritum, -ī, n., *service, kindness*.
    Quō prō meritō meō: *For this service of mine*.

5   **Augustus appellātus sum**: Octavian received the cognomen 'Augustus'
    from the Senate on January 16, 27 B.C. The title was charged with
    religious significance because the adjective **augustus, -a, -um** meant
    sacred, venerable.
    laurea, -ae, f., *laurel garland, wreath*.
    laureīs: the laurel was a sign of victory.
    aedium: here and in paragraph 35, line 3, with the meaning *home*.

6   **vestiō, -īre, -īvī, -ītum**, *to clothe, wrap*.
    vestītī: supply **sunt**.
    cīvicus, -a, -um, *civic*.
    corōnaque cīvica: this wreathe, made of oak, was symbolic of bravery in
    saving the life of a citizen.

7   **fīgō, fīgere, fīxī, fīxum**, *to fasten*.
    clupeus, -ī, m., *round shield*.
    positus: supply **est**.
    quem: the antecedent is **clupeus aureus**. The pronoun **quem** is the
    direct object of the infinitive **dare**.

8   **senātum populumque Rōmānum**: subject of the infinitive **dare**.
    clēmentia, -ae, f., *clemency*.

1 §33 Ā mē gentēs Parthōrum et Mēdōrum per lēgātōs prīncipēs
2 eārum gentium rēgēs petītōs accēpērunt. Parthī Vonōnem, rēgis
3 Phrātis fīlium, rēgis Orōdis nepōtem, Mēdī Ariobarzānem, rēgis
4 Artavazdis fīlium, rēgis Ariobarzānis nepōtem.

1 §34 In cōnsulātū sextō et septimō, postquam bella cīvīlia *takes the gen.*
2 exstīnxeram, per cōnsēnsum ūniversōrum potītus rērum
3 omnium, rem pūblicam ex meā potestāte in senātūs populīque
4 Rōmānī arbitrium trānstulī. Quō prō meritō meō senātūs
5 cōnsultō Augustus appellātus sum, et laureīs postēs aedium
6 meārum vestītī pūblicē corōnaque cīvica super iānuam meam
7 fīxa est et clupeus aureus in cūriā Iūliā positus, quem mihi   *Julian senate-house*
8 senātum populumque Rōmānum dare virtūtis clēmentiaeque et
9 iūstitiae et pietātis caussā testātum est per eius clupeī *1st perfect*
10 īnscrīptiōnem. Post id tempus auctōritāte omnibus praestitī
11 potestātis autem nihilō amplius habuī quam cēterī quī mihi
12 quōque in magistrātū conlēgae fuērunt.

---

9 **iūstitia, -ae**, f., *justice.*
    testor, -ārī, -ātus, *to testify, bear witness.*
    testātum est: translate as passive voice = *was attested to, was solemnly affirmed.* The accusative-infinitive construction is the subject of this verb.
10 **praestō, praestāre, praestitī, praestātum** + dat., *to excel, surpass.*
11 **potestātis**: partitive genitive with **amplius.**
    nihilō, adv., *in no way.*
    amplius, indecl., *more.*
    cēterī, -ae, -a, *the rest, the others.*
12 **quōque**: from **quisque.**

35

1 **tertium decimum cōnsulātum**: 2 B.C. See paragraph 22, line 8.
4 **inscrībendum**: understand **esse**.
    Aug.: abbreviation for **Augustī**.
5 **ex s. c.**: abbreviation for **ex senātūs cōnsultō**.
    cēnsuit: governing the accusative and infinitive construction **id** . . .
      īnscrībendum (esse).
    Cum scrīpsī: indicative mood in a **cum**-temporal clause.
6 **septuāgēnsumus, -a, -um**, *seventieth*.
    annum agēbam septuāgēnsumum sextum: Augustus was 76 on September 23, A.D. 13. He died on August 19, A.D. 14.

Appendix

The appendix does not form part of the inscription as composed by Augustus. It was added as a summary of expenses for the benefit of provincial readers.

1

1 **Summa pecūniae**: see paragraphs 15 through 18.
2 **dēnārium**: gen. pl.

2

1 **Opera fēcit nova**: see paragraphs 19 and 21.

3

1 **Refēcit**: see paragraph 20.

4

1 **Impēnsa**: see paragraphs 22 and 23.
    Impēnsa . . . innumerābilis: this paragraph is a predicate nominative sentence. There are two subjects, **impēnsa praestita . . . et dōnata pecūnia**. **Innumerābilis**, which agrees in gender and number with the closer subject, i.e., **pecūnia**, is the predicate adjective. The verb **erat** or **fuit** must be supplied.
    scaenicus, -a, -um, *theatrical*.
2 **naumachia, -ae**, f., *mock naval battle*.
3 **dōnāta pecūnia**: see paragraphs 15 and 16.
5 **cēnsus, -ūs**, m., *money-qualification* (of a particular social class).
    expleō, explēre, explēvī, explētum, *to fill up*.
    innumerābilis, -is, -e, *countless*.

1 §35 Tertium decimum cōnsulātum cum gerēbam, senātus et

2 equester ōrdō populusque Rōmānus ūniversus appellāvit mē

3 patrem patriae idque in vestibulō aedium meārum

4 īnscrībendum et in cūriā Iūliā et in forō Aug. sub quadrīgīs

5 quae mihi ex s.c. positae sunt cēnsuit. Cum scrīpsī haec annum

6 agēbam septuāgēnsumum sextum.

Appendix

1 §1 Summa pecūniae quam dedit vel in aerārium vel plēbēī

2 Rōmānae vel dīmissīs mīlitibus: dēnārium sexiēns mīlliēns.

1 §2 Opera fēcit nova aedem Mārtis, Iovis Tonantis et Feretrī,

2 Apollinis, dīvī Iūlī, Quirīnī, Minervae, Iūnōnis Rēgīnae, Iovis

3 Lībertātis, Larum, deum Penātium, Iuventātis, Mātris Magnae,

4 Lupercal, pulvīnar ad circum, cūriam cum Chalcidicō, Forum

5 Augustum, basilicam Iūliam, theātrum Mārcellī, porticum

6 Octāviam, nemus trāns Tiberim Caesarum.

1 §3 Refēcit Capitōlium sacrāsque aedēs numerō octōgintā duās,

2 theātrum Pompēī, aquārum rīvōs, Viam Flāminiam.

1 §4 Impēnsa praestita in spectācula scaenica et mūnera

2 gladiātōrum atque athlētās et vēnātiōnēs et naumachiam et

3 dōnāta pecūnia colōnīs, mūnicipiīs, oppidīs terrae mōtū

4 incendiōque cōnsūmptīs aut virītim amīcīs senātōribusque

5 quōrum cēnsūs explēvit, innumerābilis.

Temple of Augutstus and Roma, Ankara. Photograph courtesy of the Center for Epigraphical and Palaeographical Studies, The Ohio State University.

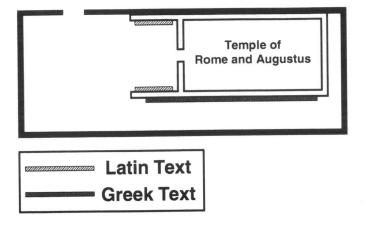

Drawing of the Temple of Augustus and Roma. After drawing by C. H. Greenwalt, photocopy courtesy of the Center for Epigraphical and Palaeographical Studies, The Ohio State University. Redrawn and edited by Tim Pieri.

Latin text of Monumentum Ancyranum. North ante. Title and paragraph §1. Photograph courtesy of the Center for Epigraphical and Palaeographical Studies, The Ohio State University.

Latin text of Monumentum Ancyranum. South ante. Columns 4–6. Photograph courtesy of the Center for Epigraphical and Palaeographical Studies, The Ohio State University.

Latin text of Monumentum Ancyranum. South ante. Paragraphs 27, 28, 29. Photograph courtesy of the Center for Epigraphical and Palaeographical Studies, The Ohio State University.

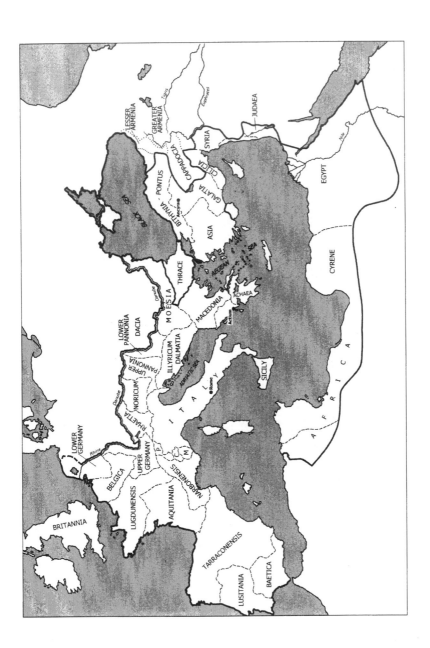

Map of the Roman empire during the reign of Augustus. After Michael Grant, *Atlas of Classical History. From 1700 B.C. to A.D. 565*, 5th ed., 1994, New York: Oxford University Press, pp. 57–58. Redrawn and edited by Tim Pieri.

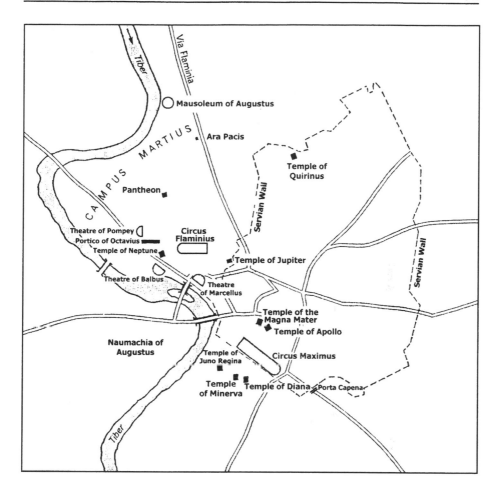

Map of the city Rome. After A. H. M. Jones, *Augustus*, 1970, New York: Norton & Co., p. 182. Redrawn and edited by Tim Pieri.

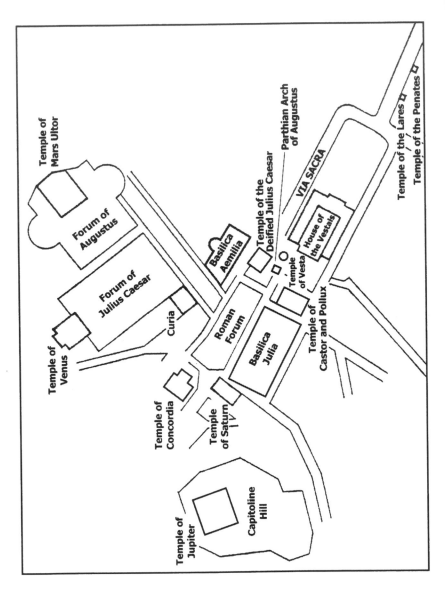

Map of the Capitolium and Roman Fora. After A. H. M. Jones, *Augustus*, 1970, New York: Norton & Co., p. 182. Redrawn and edited by Tim Pieri.

INDEX

A

Achāia, -ae, f., *Achaia*; 28.2

Actium, -ī, n., *Actium* (a promontory north of Acarnania, a state in north-west Greece); 25.5

Adiabēnī, -ōrum, m. pl., *the Adiabenians* (an Assyrian people); 32.3

Aegyptus, -ī, f., *Egypt*; 27.1

Aethiopia, -ae, f., *Aethiopia* 26.13, 26.15

Āfrica, -ae, f., *Roman province of Africa*; 25.6, 28.1

Āfricānus, -a, -um, *African*; 22.11

Agrippa, Marcus, m., son-in-law and colleague of Augustus; 8.3, 22.7

Albānī, -ōrum, m. pl., *the Albanians* (in the Caucasus); 31.5

Albis, Albis, f., *Elbe* (river in Germany); 26.4

Alpēs, Alpium, f. pl., *Alps*; 26.4

Antistius, Gāius, m., consul in 6 B.C.; 16.8–9

Apollō, Apollinis, m., *Apollo* (god of prophecy, music, poetry); 19.1, 21.2, 21.5, 24.6, Appendix 2.2

Appulēius, Sextus, m., consul in A.D. 14; 8.10–11

āra Pāx, ārae Pācis, f., *Altar of Peace*; 12.6

Arabia, -ae, f., *Arabia*; 26.13, 26.17

Arīminum, -ī, n., *Ariminum* (town in Umbria); 20.13

Ariobarzānēs, Ariobarzānis, m., *Ariobarzanes* (son of Artabazes, king of Media); 27.7, 33.4

Ariobarzānēs, Ariobarzānis, m., *Ariobarzanes* (son of Artavazes, king of Media); 33.3

Armenia, -ae, f., *Armenia*; 27.1

Armenii, -ōrum, m. pl., *the Armenians*; 27.9

Arruntius, Lūcius, m., consul in 22 B.C.; 5.2

Arruntius, Lūcius, m., consul in A.D. 6 and son of L. Arruntius (see above); 17.3

Artabazus, Artabazī, m., *Artabazus* (father of Ariobarzanes, king of Media); 27.7

Artavasdēs, Artavasdis, m., *Artavasdes* (son of Tigranes II, king of Armenia); 27.4, 32.2, 33.3

Artavasdēs, Artavasdis, m., *Artavasdes* (son of Ariobarzanes, king of Media; 27.8, 33.4

Artaxarēs, Artaxaris, m., *Artaxares* (king of the Adiabenians); 32.3

Artaxēs, Artaxis, m., *Artaxes* (son of Artavasdes, king of Armenia); 27.2

Asia, -ae, f., *Asia*; 24.1, 28.2

Asinius, Gāius, m., consul in 8 B.C.; 8.7

VOCABULARY

A

ā or **ab**, prep. + abl., *from, by*

acciō, acciere, acciī/accīvī, accītum, *to send for, invite, summon*

accipiō, accipere, accēpī, acceptum, *to accept, get, receive, welcome*

aciēs, aciēī, f., *battle*

adiciō, adicere, adiēcī, adiectum ɪ dat., *to add to*

adlegō, adlegere, adlēgī, adlēctum, *to appoint, elect*

administrō, -āre, -āvī, -ātum, *to administer*

adque = **atque,** conj., *as*

adsignō, -āre, -āvī, -ātum, *to assign*

aedēs, aedis, f., *temple; house*

aequē, adv., *equally*

aerārium, -ī, n., *public treasury*

aetās, aetātis, f., *age, lifetime*

ager, agrī, m., *field, territory, land*

agō, agere, ēgī, āctum, *to do, drive; discuss, debate*

ahēneus, -a, -um, *made of bronze*

aliquantō, adv., *to some extent, by a considerable amount*

aliquod = **aliquot,** indecl. adj., *some, several*

aliquotiēns, adv., *several times*

alius, alia, aliud, *another, other, one . . . another*

alter, altera, alterum, *another; second*

amīcitia, -ae, f., *friendship*

āmittō, āmittere, āmīsī, āmissum, *to lose*

amphitheātrum, -ī, n., *amphitheater*

ampliō, -āre, -āvī, -ātus, *to extend, increase*

amplius, indecl., *more*

amplus, -a, -um, *distinguished, eminent*

anniversārius, -a, -um, *celebrated annually, performed annually, annual*

annōna, -ae, f., *grain-supply*

annus, -ī, m., *year*

annuus, -a, -um, *annual*

ante, prep. + acc., *before, in front of*

anteā, adv., *previously, before*

appellō, -āre, -āvī, -ātum, *to call, name*

appetō, appetere, appetīvī, appetītum, *to seek after*

apsēns, apsentis, *absent*

apud, prep. + acc., *with, at the house of, in front of, before*

aqua, -ae, f., *water; aqueduct*

āra, -ae, f., *altar*

arbitrium, -ī, n., *dominion, control*

argenteus, -a, -um, *made of silver*

arma, armōrum, n. pl., *arms, weapons*

athlēta, -ae, m., *athlete*

auctor, auctōris, m., *advocate, supporter; mover, proposer (of a law)*

auctōritās, auctōritātis, f., *influence, prestige, authority*

augeō, augēre, auxī, auctum, *to increase*

augur, auguris, m., *augur, diviner*

augustus, -a, -um, *sacred, venerable*

aureus, -a, -um, *made of gold*

auspicium, -ī, n., *leadership, authority; pl., auspices*

aut, conj., *or*

autem, particle, *however, but, moreover*

B

basilica, -ae, f., *basilica* (hall used as a law-court)

bellum, -ī, n., *war*

benignē, adv., *kindly*

bēstia, -ae, f., *beast*

birēmis, -is, -e, *having two oars to each bench or room*

bis, adv., *twice*

C

cadō, cadere, cecidī, cāsum, *to fall*

caedō, caedere, cecīdī, caesum, *to cut down, slaughter*

campus, -ī, m., *plain, field*

capiō, capere, cēpī, captum, *to seize, take*

caput, capitis, n., *head*

carmen, carminis, n., *song, hymn*

cau(s)sa, -ae, f., *reason.* **causā** + gen., *for the sake of, as*

cavō, -āre, -āvī, -ātum, *to dig out*

celeber, celebris, celebre, *populous*

cēnseō, cēnsēre, cēnsuī, cēnsum, *to decree; to register/enrol* (at a census)

cēnsus, -ūs, m., *registration of Roman citizens, census; money-qualification* (of a particular social class)

centum, *a hundred*

cēterī, -ae, -a, *the rest, the others*

circiter, adv., *approximately, roughly*

citrā, prep. + acc., *on this side of*

cīvicus, -a, -um, *civic*

cīvīlis, -is, -e, *occurring between citizens, civil*

cīvis, cīvis, gen. pl., **cīvium**, m./f., *citizen*

cīvitās, cīvitātis, f., *city, town*

classis, classis, f., *fleet*

claudō, claudere, clausī, clausum, *to shut*

clēmentia, -ae, f., *clemency*

clupeus, -ī, m., *round shield*

coemō, coemere, coēmī, coēmptum, *to buy up, purchase*

coepī, coepisse, coeptum, *to begin*

cognōmen, cognōminis, n., *surname* (third or fourth name of a Roman)

cōgō, cōgere, coēgī, coāctum, *to compel, force*

collēga, -ae = conlēga, -ae, m., *partner, colleague*

conlēga, see **collēga**

collēgium, -ī, n., *college, organization*

colōnia, -ae, f., *colony, settlement*

colōnus, -ī, m., *colonist*

comitium, -ī, n., *a place of assembly;* pl., *election*

commercium, -ī, n., *exchange*

comparō, -āre, -āvī, -ātum, *to buy, obtain, get ready*

complūrēs, -ēs, -a, *several*

condō, condere, condidī, conditum, *to found, establish*

cōnferō, cōnferre, contulī, collātum, irreg., *to confer, bestow*

cōnficiō, cōnficere, cōnfēcī, cōnfectum, *to kill, destroy*

cōnflīgō, cōnflīgere, cōnflīxī, cōnflīctum, *to clash, do battle*

cōnfluō, cōnfluere, cōnflūxī, *to meet, gather, assemble*

cōnfugiō, cōnfugere, cōnfūgī, *to flee for refuge*

congiārium, -ī, n., *money distributed as a gift, largess, gratuity*

conlēga, -ae, see **collēga, -ae**

cōnsacrō, -āre, -āvī, -ātum, *to dedicate*

cōnsēnsus, -ūs, m., *consent, agreement*

cōnsentiō, cōnsentīre, cōnsēnsī,
   cōnsēnsum, *to agree*
cōnservō, -āre, -āvī, -ātum, *to*
   preserve
cōnsilium, -ī, n., *plan*
cōnstituō, cōnstituere, cōnstituī,
   cōnstitūtum, *to decide*
cōnstō, cōnstāre, cōnstitī + dat. of
   person making the expenditure, *to cost*
cōnsul, cōnsulis, m., *consul*
cōnsulāris, -is, -e, *having the status*
   of an exconsul
cōnsulātus, -ūs, m., *consulship*
cōnsultum, -ī, n., *decree*
cōnsūmō, cōnsūmere, cōnsūmpsī,
   cōnsūmptum, *to destroy; to*
   wear away; to consume
continēns, continentis + dat.,
   adjacent to, next to, close to
continenter, adv., *continuously*
continuus, -a, -um, *successive,*
   consecutive
contrā, prep. + acc., *against,*
   opposite, in front of, facing
cōpia, -ae, f., *supply;* pl. *troops,*
   forces
corōna, -ae, f., *garland, crown*
corōnārius, -a, -um, *used for*
   making crowns or wreaths
creō, -āre, -āvī, -ātum, *to appoint,*
   create, make
cum, prep. + abl., *with*
cum, conj., *when, since, whenever*
cūnctus, -a, -um, *the whole of, all*
cūra, -ae, f., *care*
cūrātiō, cūrātiōnis, f., *superinten-*
   dence, administration
cūrātor, cūrātōris, m., *supervisor,*
   superintendent, curator
currus, -ūs, m., *chariot*
curūlis, -is, -e, *curule*

D

dē, prep. + abl., *down from, from*
   concerning, about
dēbeō, -ēre, -uī, -itum, *to owe;* +
   inf., *ought*
decem, *ten*
dēcernō, dēcernere, dēcrēvī,
   dēcrētum, *to decree*
decimus, -a, -um, *tenth*
dēcrētum, -ī, n., *decree*
dēdūcō, dēdūcere, dēdūxī,
   dēductum, *to bring, escort,*
   show into
dēferō, dēferre, dētulī, dēlātum,
   to award, grant
dēficiō, dēficere, dēfēcī,
   dēfectum, *to be lacking, be*
   insufficient
deinceps, adv., *in succession*
dēnārius, -ī, m., *denarius* (silver
   coin)
dēpōnō, dēpōnere, dēposuī,
   dēpositum, *to lay down, put*
   aside, set down
dēposcō, dēposcere, dēpoposcī, *to*
   demand
dēprecor, -ārī, -ātus, *to refuse,*
   decline
dēpugnō, -āre, -āvī, -ātum, *to do*
   battle, fight in the arena
dēscīscō, dēscīscere, dēscīvī,
   dēscītum, *to revolt*
dēsignō, -āre, -āvī, -ātum, *to*
   appoint, select
dētrīmentum, -ī, n., *harm, damage*
dēvincō, dēvincere, dēvīcī,
   dēvictum, *to defeat decisively,*
   subdue
dīcō, dīcere, dīxī, dictum, *to say,*
   tell
dictātūra, -ae, f., *dictatorship*
diēs, diēī, m., *day*
dīmittō, dīmittere, dīmīsī,
   dīmissum, *to send away*

dīvus, -a, -um, *deified*
dō, dare, dedī, datum, *to give*
dominātiō, dominātiōnis, f.,
  tyranny, power
dominus, -ī, m., *master, owner*
domō, domāre, domuī, domitum,
  to subdue
dōnō, -āre, -āvī, -ātum, *to give; to*
  present somebody (acc.) *with*
  something (abl.)
dōnum, -ī, *gift*
ducentī, -ae, -a, *two hundred*
duo, duae, duo, *two*
duodecim, *twelve*
duodecimum, adv., *for the twelfth*
  time
duodēvīcēnsimum, adv., *for the*
  eighteenth time
duplicō, -āre, -āvī, -ātum, *to*
  double (the capacity of)
dux, ducis, m., *leader*

E

ēdō, ēdere, ēdidī, ēditum, *to give*
  out
ego, personal pro., *I*
ēmereō, -ēre, -uī, -itum, *to serve*
  out, complete
ēmētior, ēmētīrī, ēmēnsus, *to*
  measure out, distribute by
  measure
emō, emere, ēmī, ēmptum, *to buy*
epulō, epulōnis, m., *banqueter,*
  diner
eques, equitis, m., *knight* (social
  class with minimum property
  qualification of 400,000
  sesterces)
equester, equestris, equestre,
  equestrian, going on horseback
ēripiō, ēripere, ēripuī, ēreptum,
  to snatch from, rescue
et, conj., *and, also.* **et . . . et,** conj.,
  both . . . and

etiam, particle, *now, yet, still*
ex or **ē,** prep. + abl., *from, out of*
excīdō, excīdere, excīdī, excīsum,
  to destroy, exterminate
exemplar, exemplāris, n., *copy*
exemplum, -ī, n., *example;* pl.,
  exemplary practices, models of
  conduct
exercitus, -ūs, m., *army*
exilium, -ī, n., *exile*
expellō, expellere, expulsī,
  expulsum, *to drive out, expel*
ex(s)tō, exstāre, exstitī, *to exist*
exolēscō, exolēscere, exolēvī,
  exolētum, *to fade away, die out*
experior, experīrī, expertus, *to*
  test, try
expleō, explēre, explēvī,
  explētum, *to fill up*
externus, -a, -um, *foreign*
extinguō, extinguere, exstīnxī,
  exstīnctum, *to put out,*
  extinguish

F

facinus, facinoris, n., *crime*
faciō, facere, fēcī, factum, *to make,*
  do; cause, bring about
fascēs, fascium, m. pl., *rods*
  (symbols of office)
ferē, adv., *almost*
ferō, ferre, tulī, lātum, *to bear,*
  carry; to pass a law
fētiālis, fētiālis, m., *fetial priest*
fidēs, fideī, f., *good faith, reliability,*
  trust
fīgō, fīgere, fīxī, fīxum, *to fasten*
fīlius, -ī, m., *son*
fīnis, fīnis, gen. pl., **fīnium,** m.,
  boundary, limit
fīnitimus, -a, -um, *situated/living on*
  the boundary; adjacent to + dat.
fīō, fierī, factus sum, irreg., *to*
  become, be made, be done, happen

flūmen, flūminis, n., *river*

fortūna, -ae, f., *fortune* (good or bad)

frāter, frātris, m., *brother*

frequēns, frequentis, *densely packed, crowded*

frūmentārius, -a, -um, *consisting of grain*

frūmentātiō, frūmentātiōnis, f., *distribution of grain; a ration of grain*

frūmentum, -ī, n., *corn, grain*

fugiō, fugere, fūgī, *to flee*

G

gener, generī, m., *son-in-law*

gēns, gentis, gen. pl., **gentium**, f., *family, clan*

gerō, gerere, gessī, gestum, *to carry, wear; bear; administer, conduct, manage*

gladiātōrius, -a, -um, *gladiatorial*

grandis, -is, -e, *great*

H

habeō, -ēre, -uī, -itum, *to have, hold*

hasta, -ae, f., *spear*

hērēs, hērēdis, m., *heir*

hic, haec, hoc, *this, the latter*

homō, hominis, m., *man*

honōrificus, -a, -um, *bestowing honor*

honōs, honōris, m., *honor*

horreum, -ī, n., *granary*

hostis, hostis, gen. pl., **hostium**, m., *enemy*

I

iam, adv., *now, already*

iānua, -ae, f., *door*

īdem, eadem, idem, *the same*

ignōscō, ignōscere, ignōvī, ignōtum + dat., *to pardon, forgive*

ille, illa, illud, *that; he, she, it; the former*

imitor, -ārī, -ātus, *to imitate, copy*

immortālis, -is, -e, *immortal*

impendō, impendere, impendī, impēnsum, *to pay out, spend*

impēnsa, -ae, f., *expense*

imperātor, imperātōris, m., *commander, emperor*

imperium, -ī, n., *empire, power*

in, prep. + abl., *in, on, among*

in, prep. + acc., *into, against*

incendium, -ī, n., *fire*

incīdō, incīdere, incīsī, incīsum, *to engrave, inscribe*

inclūdō, inclūdere, inclūsī, inclūsum, *to bound, surround, enclose; to incorporate, insert*

incohō, -āre, -āvī, -ātum, *to start work on*

ineō, inīre, iniī or inīvī, initum, irreg., *to go into, enter*

īnferō, īnferre, intulī, illātum, irreg., *to bring in.* **bellum īnferre** + dat., *to make war upon*

innumerābilis, -is, -e, *countless*

īnscrīptiō, īnscrīptiōnis, f., *inscription*

īnsequor, īnsequī, īnsecūtus, *to follow after*

intersum, interesse, interfuī + dat., *to take part in*

intrā, prep. + acc., *inside*

iniūria, -ae, f., *unjust treatment*

interficiō, interficere, interfēcī, interfectum, *to kill*

ipse, ipsa, ipsum, *himself, herself, itself, themselves, very*

is, ea, id, *he, she, it; this, that*

ita, adv., *thus, so, in this way, in such a way*

item, adv., *also*

iterum, adv., *again, a second time*

iubeō, iubēre, iussī, iussum, *to order*

iūdicium, -ī, n., *legal proceedings*

iūrō, -āre, -āvī, -ātum, *to swear* (as in an oath)

iussus, -ūs, m., *order*

iūstitia, -ae, f., *justice*

iuvenis, iuvenis, m., *young man*

iuventūs, iuventūtis, f., *youth*

iuvō, iuvāre, iūvī, iūtum, *to assist*

L

lābor, lābī, lāpsus, *to slip, fall, stumble*

lātitūdō, lātitūdinis, f., *width*

laurea, -ae, f., *laurel garland, wreath*

laurus, -ī, m., *bay (tree)*

lēgātiō, lēgātiōnis, f., *embassy*

lēgātus, -ī, m., *envoy*

lēgitimus, -a, -um, *lawful*

legō, legere, lēgī, lēctum, *to choose, select, pick;* here, *to revise the membership of*

lēx, lēgis, f., *law*

līberī, -ōrum, m. pl., *children*

līberō, -āre, -āvī, -ātum, *to set free*

lībertās, lībertātis, f., *freedom*

lībra, -ae, f., *a balance, pair of scales; a pound* (measure of weight)

locus, -ī, m., *rank, position, precedence;* n. in pl., *places*

longitūdō, longitūdinis, f., *length*

lūdus, -ī, m., *school, game;* pl., *games*

lūdī saec(u)lārēs, lūdōrum saec(u)lārium, m. pl., *secular games*

lūstrum, -ī, n., *lustration, ceremony of purification*

M

magister, magistrī, m., *schoolmaster, master, captain*

magistrātus, -ūs, m., *magistracy*

magnus, -a, -um, *big, great, large*

maior, maior, maius, gen., maiōris, *bigger.* maiōrēs, maiōrum, m. pl., *ancestors*

mālō, mālle, māluī, irreg., *to prefer*

manibiae, -ārum, f. pl., *booty, spoils*

mare, maris, gen. pl., marium, n., *sea*

maximus, -a, -um, *biggest, greatest, very great, very large*

memoria, -ae, f., *memory*

meritum, -ī, n., *service, kindness*

metus, -ūs, m., *fear*

meus, -a, -um, *my, mine*

mīles, mīlitis, m., *soldier*

mīlitāris, -is, -e, *of the military*

mīlitia, -ae, f., *military service*

mīlitō, -āre, -āvī, -ātum, *to perform military service, serve* (as a soldier)

mīlle, *a thousand.* mīllia, mīllium, n. pl., *thousands*

mīlliēns, adv., *one thousand times*

minor, minor, minus, gen., minōris, *smaller*

mittō, mittere, mīsī, missum, *to send, let go*

mors, mortis, gen. pl., mortium, f., *death*

mortuus, -a, -um, *dead*

mōs, mōris, m., *custom, usage, fashion;* pl., *conduct, behavior, morals, character*

mōtus, -ūs, m., *civil disorder, disturbance*

multitūdō, multitūdinis, f., *crowd*

multus, -a, -um, *much;* pl., *many*

mūnicipātim, adv., *by municipalities*

mūnicipium, -ī, n., *community, municipality, town*

mūnus, mūneris, n., *gift, service, gladiatorial show;* pl., *games*

N

nāscor, nāscī, nātus, *to be born*
naumachia, -ae, f., *mock naval battle*
nāvālis, -is, -e, *involving ships*
nāvēs, nāvis, gen. pl., **nāvium,** f., *ship*
nāvigō, -āre, -āvī, -ātum, *to sail*
nē, conj. + subjunctive, *not to, so that . . . not*
nēmō, nēminis, m. / f., *no one*
nemus, nemoris, n., *woods, forest, grove*
nepōs, nepōtis, m., *grandson*
nihilō, adv., *in no way*
nōmen, nōminis, n., *name*
nōn, adv., *not*
nōngentī, -ae, -a, *nine hundred*
noster, nostra, nostrum, *our*
novem, *nine*
novus, -a, -um, *new*
nūllus, -a, -um, *no, none*
numerus, -ī, m., *number*
numerātum, -ī, n., *cash, money*
numerō, -āre, -āvī, -ātum, *to count, number, include*
nummārius, -a, -um, *consisting of money*
nummus, -ī, m., *sesterce* (denomination of Roman coinage)
nunc, adv., *now*
nuncupō, -āre, -āvī, -ātum, *to utter, pronounce*
nunquam = numquam, adv., *never*

O

ob, prep. + acc., *on account of*
obviam, adv. + dat., *so as to meet*
occāsiō, occāsiōnis, f., *convenient circumstance, opportunity*

occupō, -āre, -āvī, -ātum, *to seize, take possession of*
octōgintā, *eighty*
omnīnō, adv., *in every respect, all told, altogether*
omnis, -is, -e, *all, the whole, every, each*
oppidum, -ī, n., *town*
opprimō, oppimere, oppressī, oppressum, *to overwhelm*
opus, operis, n., *work, product*
orbis, orbis, gen. pl. **orbium,** m., *circle*
orbis terrārum, *the circle of the lands, the whole earth*
ōrdō, ōrdinis, m., *order, rank, class*
orior, orīrī, ortus, *to rise*
oriundus, -a, -um, *descended from*
ōrnāmentum, -ī, n., *ornament; religious relic*
ōstium, -ī, n., *mouth* (of a river)
ovo, -āre, -āvī, -ātum, *to celebrate an ovation*

P

pācō, -āre, -āvī, -ātum, *to bring under control*
parcō, parcere, pepercī + dat., *to spare*
parēns, parentis, m. / f., *parent*
pareō, -ēre, -uī, paritum + dat., *to obey*
pariō, parere, peperī, partum, *to give birth to, bear; to bring forth, produce; to procure, get, obtain*
parma, -ae, f., *small, round shield*
pars, partis, gen. pl., **partium,** f., *part, direction, region*
pater, patris, m., *father*
patior, patī, passus, *to suffer, endure, permit*
patria, -ae, f., *nation, native land, country*

patriciī, -ōrum, m. pl., *patricians,
nobility*
patrimōnium, -ī, n., *inheritence*
paucī, -ae, -a, *few*
paullō = paulō, adv., *a little*
pāx, pācis, f., *peace*
pecūnia, -ae, f., *money*
pedester, pedestris, pedestre,
pedestrian, going on foot
penetrālis, penetrālis, n., *inner
shrine*
pēnūria, -ae, f., *shortage, scarcity*
per, prep. + acc., *through, along*
perferō, perferre, pertulī,
perlātum, *to submit to, endure*
perficiō, perficere, perfēcī,
perfectum, *to accomplish*
perīclum, -ī, n., *danger*
pernumerō, -āre, -āvī, -ātum, *to
count out, pay over*
perpetuus, -a, -um, *lasting,
permanent*
persolvō, persolvere, persolvī,
persolūtum, *to give/pay out*
perveniō, pervenīre, pervēnī,
perventum + ad + acc., *to
arrive at, reach*
pēs, pedis, m., *foot*
petō, petere, petiī or petīvi,
petītum, *to look for, seek, head
for, aim at, attack*
pignus, pignoris, n., *pledge, surety,
guarantee*
pīla, -ae, f., *pillar*
plēbēs, plēbēī, also plēbī, m.,
plebeians, people
plēbs, plēbis, m., *plebeians, people*
plūs, plūris, n., *more*
pondō, adv., *in weight, by weight*
pōnō, pōnere, posuī, positum, *to
put, place*
pōns, pontis, m., *bridge*
pontifex, pontificis, m., *Roman
high-priest*
populus, -ī, m., *people*

porta, -ae, f., *gate*
porticus, -ūs, f., *colonnade, portico*
possideō, possidēre, possēdī,
possessum, *to appropriate*
possum, posse, potuī, irreg., *to be
able; can*
post, prep. + acc., *after*
posteā, adv., *afterward*
posterī, -ōrum, m. pl., *posterity,
descendants*
postis, postis, gen pl., postium,
m., *door-post*
potestās, potestātis, f., *control,
power*
potior, potīrī, potītus, *to obtain,
seize*
praebeō, -ēre, -uī, *to display, show,
provide*
praedium, -ī, n., *portion of land*
praedō, praedōnis, m., *pirate*
praemium, -ī, n., *reward, recompense*
praesēns, praesentis, *present*
praestō, praestāre, praestitī,
praestātum + dat., *to excel,
surpass*
praesum, praeesse, praefuī + dat.,
to be in charge of
praeter, prep. + acc., *except*
praetermittō, praetermittere,
praetermīsī, praetermissum,
to leave out, omit, neglect
praetor, praetōris, m., *praetor
(public official in charge of
judicial proceedings)*
prīmus, -a, -um, *first*
prīnceps, prīncipis, *leading*
prīnceps, prīncipis, m., *emperor,
leader, leading citizen*
prior, prior, prius, gen., priōris,
first (of two), previous
prīvignus, -ī, m., *stepson*
prīvātim, adv., *in private, personally*
prīvātus, -a, -um, *one's own,
private*
prō, prep. + abl., *for, on behalf of, as*

prōcēdō, prōcēdere, prōcessī,
prōcessum, *to go forward*
prōdō, prōdere, prōdidī,
prōditum + memoriae, *to
hand down, record*
proelium, -ī, *fight, battle*
prōferō, prōferre, prōtulī,
prōlātum, irreg., *to carry
forward, continue*
prōflīgō, -āre, -āvī, -ātum, *to be in
a nearly completed state*
prō praetōre, m. indecl., *propraetor*
prosperē, adv., *successfully*
prōvideō, prōvidēre, prōvīdī,
prōvīsum, *to see in advance, see
beforehand*
prōvincia, -ae, f., *province*
prōvinciālis, -is, -e, *of a province*
proximus, -a, -um, *nearby*
pūblicus, -a, -um, *public*
pugnō, -āre, -āvī, -ātum, *to fight*
pulvīnar, pulvīnāris, n., *sacred
couch*

Q

quā, rel. adv., *wherever*
quadrāgēnsimus, -a, -um, *fortieth*
quadrāgiēns, adv., *forty times*
quadrāgintā, *forty*
quadrīga, -ae, f., *chariot with its
team of four horses*
quadringēnī, -ae, -a, *four hundred
each/apiece*
quam, adv., *than, as*
quantus, -a, -um, *how big? how
much?*
quārtus, -a, -um, *fourth*
quater, adv., *four times*
quattuor, *four*
-que, enclitic conj., *and*
quī, quae, quod, *who, which, that*
quīngentī, -ae, -a, *five hundred*
quīngentiēns, adv., *five hundred
times*

quīnquāgiēns, adv., *fifty times*
quīnquāgintā, *fifty*
quīnquiēns, adv., *five times*
quīnquennium, -ī, n., *a period of
five years*
quīntum, adv., *for the fifth time*
quīntus, -a, -um, *fifth*
quis, qua/quae, quid, indef. adj.,
some, any
quis, quid, *who?, what?* nē quis,
quid, *lest anyone, anything*
quisquam, quisquam, quicquam,
any
quisque, quaeque, quodque, adj.,
every, each
quō, rel. adv., *to which place*
quoad, rel. adv., *for as long as,
while*
quoque, adv., *also*
quotiēnscumque, conj., *as often as*

R

rebellō, -āre, -āvī, -ātum, *to rebel*
recipiō, recipere, recēpī,
receptum, *to receive, recapture*
reciperō (= recuperō), -āre, -āvī,
-ātum, *to recover*
recūsō, -āre, -āvī, -ātum, *to reject*
(the proposition/idea that +
nē + subjunctive)
reddō, reddere, reddidī,
redditum, *to give back, return*
redeō, redīre, rediī or redīvī,
reditum, irreg., *to return, go
back*
reditus, -ūs, m., *return*
regiō, regiōnis, f., *region*
rēgnum, -ī, n., *kingdom*
regō, regere, rēxī, rēctum, *to rule*
rēmex, rēmigis, m., *rower*
remittō, remittere, remīsī,
remissum, *to send back*
repōnō, repōnere, reposuī,
repositum, *to put back*

rēs, reī, f., *thing, matter, situation, affair*

rēs gestae, rērum gestārum, f. pl., *accomplishments*

rēs pūblica, reī pūblicae, f., *republic, the state*

rēx, rēgis, m., *king*

rīpa, -ae, f., *bank* (of a river)

rīvus, -ī, m., *conduit, channel, watercourse*

rōstrātus, -a, -um, *provided with a beak*

S

sacerdōs, sacerdōtis, m., *priest*

sacerdōtium, -ī, n., *priesthood*

sacra, -ōrum, n. pl., *religious rites, sacrifice*

sacrāmentum, -ī, n., *military oath of allegiance*

sacrificium, -ī, n., *sacrifice*

sacrōsānctus, -a, -um, *inviolable*

saeculum, -ī, n., *generation*

saepe, adv., *often*

saliāris, -is, -e, *of the Salii* (a college of twelve priests dedicated to the service of Mars)

scaenicus, -a, -um, *theatrical*

scrībō, scrībere, scrīpsī, scrīptum, *to write*

sē, reflexive pro., *himself, herself, oneself, itself, themselves*

semel, adv., *once, one time*

senātor, senātōris, m., *senator*

senātus, -ūs, m., *Senate*

sententia, -ae, f., *opinion*

septem, *seven*

septimum, adv., *for the seventh time*

septingentiēns, adv., *seven hundred times*

septuāgēnsumus, -a, -um, *seventieth*

servīlis, -is, -e, *of slaves*

servus, -ī, m., *slave*

sescentī, -ae, -a, *six hundred*

sescentiēns, adv., *six hundred times*

sēstertius, -ī, m., *sesterce* (denomination of Roman coinage)

sexāgēnī, -ae, -a, *sixty each/apiece*

sexāgintā, *sixty*

sexsiēns = sexiēns, adv., *sixty times*

sextum, adv., *for the sixth time*

sextus, -a, -um, *sixth*

sī, conj., *if*

signum, -ī, n., *military standard*

simul, adv., *together, at the same time*

sine, prep. + abl., *without*

singulī, -ae, -a, *one apiece*

sodālis, sodālis, m., *member of a society/fraternity/priesthood*

solum, -ī, n., *foundation, base; ground; property*

sōlus, -a, -um, *alone*

solvō, solvere, solvī, solūtum, *to loosen, untie*

spectāclum, -ī, *show, spectacle*

spoliō, -āre, -āvī, -ātum, *to plunder, pillage*

spolium, -ī, n., *spoils* (arms, equipment taken from a defeated enemy)

statua, -ae, f., *statue*

stīpendium, -ī, n., *military service*

stō, stāre, stetī, statum, *to stand*

sub, prep. + abl., *under, beneath*

subiciō, subicere, subiēcī, subiectum, *to place underneath/below;* + dat., *to make subject to*

suscipiō, suscipere, suscēpī, susceptum, *to undertake* (an oath, a vow)

sum, esse, fuī, irreg., *to be*

summa, -ae, f., *total number/amount*

summus, summa, summum, *greatest, very great, highest*

sūmo, sūmere, sūmpsī, sūmptum, *to take, take up, pick out*

superō, -āre, -āvī, -ātum, *to overcome*

supersedeō, supersedēre, supersēdī, supersessum + dat. or abl., *to abstain from; to pass over*

supplex, supplicis, m., *suppliant*

supplicium, -ī, n., *punishment*

supplicō, -āre, -āvī, -ātum + dat., *to worship; to make thank offerings (to); to pray; to make propritiatory offerings (to)*

suus, -a, -um, *his, her, one's, its, their (own)*

T

templum, -ī, n., *temple*

tempus, temporis, n., *time*

ter, adv., *three times*

terdeciēns, adv., *thirteen times*

terra, -ae, f., *earth, ground, land*

tertium, adv., *for a third time*

testāmentum, -ī, n., *will, testament*

testor, -ārī, -ātus, *to testify, bear witness*

theātrum, -ī, n., *theater*

titulus, -ī, m., *commemorative inscription*

tollō, tollere, sustulī, sublātum, *to remove*

tōtus, -a, -um, *all, the whole*

tractus, tractūs, m., *region*

trādō, trādere, trādidī, trāditum, *to hand over*

trāns, prep. + acc., *across*

trānsgredior, trānsgredī, trānsgressus, *to cross*

trecēnī, -ae, -a, *three hundred each/ apiece*

trecentī, -ae, -a, *three hundred*

trēs, trēs, tria, *three*

tribūnicius, -a, -um, *tribunician*

tribuō, tribuere, tribuī, tribūtum, *to award, grant, bestow*

tribūtus, -ūs, m., *allocation, apportionment, distribution*

trīcēnsimum, adv., *for the thirtieth time*

trīgintā, *thirty*

trirēmis, trirēmis, f., *trireme* (ship with three banks of oars)

triumphālis, -is, -e, *triumphal*

triumphō, -āre, -āvī, -ātum, *to celebrate a triumph*

triumphus, -ī, m., *triumphal procession*

triumvir, -ī, m., *triumvir*

trucīdō, -āre, -āvī, -ātum, *to butcher, massacre, slaughter*

tum, adv., *at that moment, then.* tum . . . tum, adv., *at one time . . . at another time; sometimes . . . sometimes*

tuto, adv., *safely, securely*

U

ulcīscor, ulcīscī, ultus, *to avenge, punish*

ūllus, -a, -um, *any*

ultrā, prep. + acc., *on the farther side of, beyond*

ultrō, adv., *on one's own initiative, of one's own accord*

ūnanimiter, adv., *with one purpose/ accord*

ūndēvīgintī, *nineteen*

ūndecimum, adv., *for the eleventh time*

undique, adv., *on all sides, from all sides*

ūniversus, -a, -um, *the whole of, the entire*

urbānus, -a, -um, *of the city/town*

urbs, urbis, gen. pl., urbium, f., *city*

ut, conj. + subj., *so that, that, to*

uterque, utraque, utrumque, *each* (of two), *both*

V

valētūdō, valētūdinis, f., *health*
vectīgāl, vectīgālis, n., *revenue* (derived from public property), *income*
vel, conj., *or.* vel . . . vel, *either . . . or*
vēnātiō, vēnātiōnis, f., *animal-hunt*
venia, -ae, f., *pardon, forgiveness*
verbum, -ī, n., *word*
vergō, -ere, *to look to, point towards*
vestibulum, -ī, n., *entrance passage*
vestiō, -īre, -īvī, -ītum, *to clothe, wrap*
vetustās, vetustātis, f., *old age*
via, -ae, f., *road, way, street*

vicem, prep. + preceding gen., *in place of, on behalf of*
vīcēnī, -ae, -a, *twenty apiece*
vīciēns, adv., *twenty times*
victor, victōris, m., *conqueror, victor*
victōria, -ae, f., *victory*
videō, vidēre, vīdī, vīsum, *to see*
vīgintī, *twenty*
vincō, vincere, vīcī, victum, *to conquer, win*
vindicō, -āre, -āvī, -ātum, *to deliver, free, liberate*
vir, -ī, m., *man, husband*
virgō, virginis, f., *maiden*
virītim, adv., *per man, individually*
vīvō, vīvere, vīxī, vīctum, *to live*
vīvus, -a, -um, *living*
volō, velle, voluī, irreg., *to wish, want, be willing*
vōtum, -ī, n., *vow, promise*

Ideal introductions and valuable field companions for navigating Rome, the ancient city

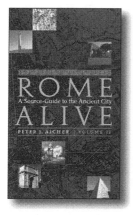

Rome Alive
A Source-Guide to the Ancient City (Vol I)
Peter J. Aicher
xxxii + 344 pp (2004) Paperback ISBN 978-0-86516-473-4

Whether you're an armchair tourist, are visiting Rome for the first time, or are a veteran of the city's charms, travelers of all ages and stages will benefit from this fascinating guidebook to Rome's ancient monuments. *Rome Alive* describes the Site and Foundation of Rome, Walls and Aqueducts, the Capitoline Hill, the Roman Forum, the Upper Sacra Via, the Palatine Hill, the Colosseum Area, the Imperial Fora, the Campus Martius, the Forum Boarium and Aventine, and the Circus Maximus to Tomb of Scipios, all using the words of the ancients who knew them best. Aicher's commentary orients the visitor to each site's ancient significance. Photographs, maps, and floorplans abound, all making this a one-of-a-kind guide. Volume II, available separately, includes the sources in Greek and Latin and is available for scholars who want access to the original texts.

Features: • Introduction with information on ancient authors cited • Latin and Greek sources, in translation • Organization by site, with commentary and notes to supplement original sources • Plenty of photographs, maps, and floorplans • General index

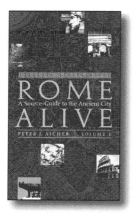

Rome Alive
A Source-Guide to the Ancient City (Vol II)
Peter J. Aicher
xii + 212 pp (2004) Paperback ISBN 978-0-86516-507-6

Rome Alive, Volume II is a companion to Volume I, aimed at the scholar-traveler who wants access to the Latin and Greek original sources translated into English in Volume I. This unique original-language guide to ancient Rome's monuments gathers together compelling observations of the ancient authors who witnessed Rome's zenith. Key maps from Volume I are included.

Review (Vols. I & II)
A book or books such as these two volumes by Peter Aicher have been needed for years. The last useful compendium of ancient literary and epigraphical sources on the city of Rome and her monuments in antiquity, translated from the original Latin and Greek, was Donald R. Dudley's *Urbs Roma* (London & Aberdeen: Phaidon, 1967) which has been out of print for decades; the last good anthology of those same sources in the original languages—the rather elegant *Breviarium Urbis Romae Antiquae* edited by A. Van Heck (Leyden: E. J. Brill, 1977)—also fell out of print some years ago. Aicher's two volumes now replace both, and do so efficiently and effectively. Volume I contains the great majority of important sources in English translation, interspersed with a few black and white photographs and rather more (and more useful) maps, site plans, and reconstruction drawings. Volume II has most of the same passages in the original languages, interspersed with a selection of 22 maps and plans chosen from the 61 illustrations included in Volume I.

– **James C. Anderson Jr.**, University of Georgia
The Classical Outlook

BOLCHAZY-CARDUCCI PUBLISHERS, INC.
WWW.BOLCHAZY.COM

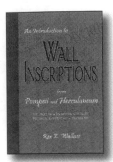

An Introduction to Wall Inscriptions
from Pompeii and Herculaneum
By Rex E. Wallace
xivi + 138 pp (2005) Paperback ISBN 978-0-86516-570-0

This edition is a representative selection of the various types of inscriptions, from political manifestos to gladiatorial announcements, found in
the ancient Roman cities of Pompeii and Herculaneum. These inscriptions,
painted and incised on the walls of public and private buildings, document
aspects of daily life in the first century AD Inscriptions, particularly graffiti,
were often written by less educated members of society, and as such provide
a rare glimpse of common Latin.

Review

Nihil durare potest tempore perpetuo... "Nothing can last forever." The anonymous first century C.E. Pom-
peian graffitist who wrote this, the first of a four-line verse on how quickly love's passion can evaporate,
has poignantly captured the problem scholars constantly face in the preservation of the written word
from antiquity. The ephemeral nature of dipinti (painted wall inscriptions) and wall graffiti (writings
incised with a sharp object or stylus) lends a certain urgency to our need to study them.

Among the treasures preserved by the eruption of Mount Vesuvius in 79 C.E. that buried Pompeii and
Herculaneum were more that 11,000 incised and painted inscriptions. While most of these are in Latin,
we can also find inscriptions in Etruscan, Greek, and Oscan. These finds make the ancient cities on the
Bay of Naples one of classical antiquity's most precious epigraphic resources.

The bulk of the dipinti and graffiti are preserved in volume IV of the *Corpus Inscriptionum Latinarum*
(CIL). For anyone who has tried to use the CIL, Rex E. Wallace's new introduction to wall inscriptions is a
most welcome teaching aid. The book developed out of undergraduate and graduate courses at the University of Massachusetts, Amherst, was fieldtested by students, and is aimed at teachers and students of
Latin who might wish to learn more about Latin written by the less educated member: of Roman society.
Classicists, historians, linguists, and students in most fields of Classical Studies will find the volume a
valuable resource.

– **Ann Olga Koloski-Ostrow**
New England Classical Journal 32.4 (2005)

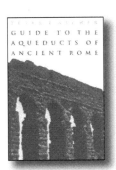

Guide to the Aqueducts
of Ancient Rome
By Peter J. Aicher
Illus., xiii + 183 pp. (1995)
Paperback, ISBN 978-0-86516-282-2
Hardbound, ISBN 978-0-86516-271-6

Aicher's work is a unique fusion of tour guide and archaelogical handbook,
allowing the reader to view the Eternal City from the vantage point of an
unmistakable yet overlooked feature of its topography.

Features: • maps • schematics drawings • photographs • reprints of
famous line drawings

Reviews

Aicher's book provides something that has not previously been available and does it with thoroughness,
readability, and accuracy . . . Aicher's guide deserves much praise and is remarkably useful. He has
earned the thanks of all who love the *ruderi* of Rome and of the Campagna for making one class of ruins
far more readily accessible and intelligible. Anyone wanting to visit the aqueducts from now on must use
it; any teacher wishing to present Roman hydraulic engineering—one of the greatest achievements of
Roman technology—to her or his students would be well-advised to start here.

– **James C. Anderson, Jr.,** University of Georgia

Guide to the Aqueducts is engaging, well presented, and well illustrated . . . Of interest to high school teachers as well as to college and university professors and travelers.

– **Gilbert Lawall,** University of Massachusetts-Amherst

BOLCHAZY-CARDUCCI PUBLISHERS, INC.
www.BOLCHAZY.com